70 DAYS
70 WAYS
He Speaks to Me

70 DAYS
70 WAYS
He Speaks to Me

bianca chandler

BMcTALKS Press
4980 South Alma School Road
Suite 2-493
Chandler, Arizona 85248

Copyright © 2020 by Bianca Chandler. All rights reserved.

No part of this publication may be reproduced, stored in a retrieval system, or transmitted in any form or by any means, electronic, mechanical, photocopying, recording, scanning, or otherwise without the prior written permission of the Publisher. Requests to the Publisher for permissions should be submitted to the Permissions Department, BMcTALKS Press, 4980 S. Alma School Road, Ste 2-493, Chandler, AZ 85248 or at www.bmctalkspress.com/permissions

The views expressed in this publication are those of the author; are the responsibility of the author; and do not necessarily reflect or represent the views of BMcTALKS Press, its owner, or its independent contractors.

Scripture quotations are taken from the Holy Bible, New Living Translation, copyright ©1996, 2004, 2015 by Tyndale House Foundation. Used by permission of Tyndale House Publishers, a Division of Tyndale House Ministries, Carol Stream, Illinois 60188. All rights reserved.

Volume pricing is available to bulk orders placed by corporations, associations, and others. For details, please contact BMcTALKS Press at info@bmtpress.com or 202.630.1218.

FIRST EDITION

Library of Congress Control Number: 2020907135

ISBN: 978-0-9998901-5-8

Printed in the United States of America.

table of contents

	DEDICATION	ix
	A LETTER TO READERS	xi
day1.	KNOW YOUR PLACE	15
day2.	DO YOU BELIEVE IN MAGIC?	19
day3.	WHILE YOU WERE OUT	21
day4.	LOYALTY, LOYALTY, LOYALTY	23
day5.	YOU'RE IN GOOD HANDS	25
day6.	COMPLETELY	27
day7.	OPEN DOORS	31
day8.	ARE YOU A TWO-CENT CHRISTIAN?	33
day9.	ACCEPTING WHAT GOD ALLOWS	37
day10.	QUICK QUESTION(S)	41
day11.	WHISPER "WOW"	45
day12.	HE IS WORKING	49
day13.	GET RIGHT OR GET LEFT	51
day14.	WHERE TO GO	55
day15.	MAY THE ODDS BE EVER IN YOUR FAVOR	59
day16.	HOW DO YOU SEE IT?	63
day17.	GROW UP	67
day18.	WHO YOU WIT?!	71
day19.	TRUSTING IN TRIBULATION	75
day20.	WHEN WISDOM IS A WOMAN	81

day21.	ALL WE NEED IS LOVE	85
day22.	WHO'S TO BLAME?	89
day23.	A STARVING SPIRIT	93
day24.	IT ALL MEANS NOTHING	97
day25.	GLORY STORY	101
day26.	AND LEAD US NOT …	103
day27.	MEEK ISN'T WEEK, HUMBLE DOESN'T GRUMBLE	107
day28.	MIRROR POWER	111
day29.	WHAT DOES YOUR HEART ASK FOR?	113
day30.	CONSTANT CONTENTMENT	117
day31.	LOCKED AND LOADED	121
day32.	CHAOS	125
day33.	SO GLAD	127
day34.	A QUICK REMINDER	129
day35.	TEARS	133
day36.	BEING THE BEST YOU	135
day37.	EVEN WHEN YOU DON'T KNOW WHY	137
day38.	MAKE IT COUNT!	139
day39.	BE GREAT!	141
day40.	RISE UP	143
day41.	BUT HOW TO DO IT?	147
day42.	MINI-MONY	151
day43.	THE ROYAL STANDARD	153
day44.	IT'S YOUR THING	157
day45.	WAIT…IT'S WORTH IT	161
day46.	AND I WONDER, WHO'S LOVING YOU?	165
day47.	IN DARKNESS COMES LIGHT	167
day48.	DEFINERS	171
day49.	OCEANS	173

day50.	TURNING WOUNDS INTO WISDOM	175
day51.	CHANGING COMPLAINTS TO CLAIMS	177
day52.	LET YOUR SPARK IGNITE	179
day53.	MOUNTAIN HIGH, VALLEY LOW	183
day54.	SUCCESS IS…	187
day55.	WHO AREYOU REALLY?	191
day56.	YOU.	193
day57.	TRY. STRIVE. THRIVE.	195
day58.	JUST BLOOM	199
day59.	WHY CAN'T YOU WALK?	203
day60.	IN THE SWING OF THINGS	207
day61.	MISSION AND MOTIVE	209
day62.	LIFE IS ART	211
day63.	BREAK FREE	213
day64.	TIGHTROPE	215
day65.	WAR CRY	217
day66.	LIVE FOR LEGACY	221
day67.	BRICK HOUSE	225
day68.	PROTECT YORU SPACE	229
day69.	YOUR JUNK IS SHOWING	233
day70.	RE-UP	237
	ABOUT THE AUTHOR	241
	MORE FROM bianca chandler	259

dedication

This book is dedicated to my amazing parents who greeted the challenge of my extraness as a blessing and never a burden. I am forever grateful for their cultivation, encouragement, and eternal love. I love you more than you will ever know.

a letter to readers

Amazing things can come from the most unexpected places. This book is a collection of reflections, analogies, stories, and conversations I have had with God. In 2016, I began to write a blog for believers. I had just come out a depression. I had found myself on the bathroom floor when a wave of depression hit hard enough to ground me. The moment when I realized without being a student, maintaining a routine that I had for years upon years of my life, that besides being a devout Christian, I had "no identity." The only things still on my schedule were church-related. I remember feeling like "Who am I in addition to being a person who goes to church?" So I asked God, and He answered with "That is enough. Everything else you will ever be will always be because of me!"

In that moment, I made the decision that was enough for me and surrendered fully to whatever was His will or plan. I rededicated myself, my identity, my works, my life. Immediately after, I shifted how I spent time with God. In the next few months, He deposited ministries in me to birth for leading other people closer to Christ as well.

I wanted to create a space that was relatable with concepts that were easy to grasp and, consequently, make a relationship with God easier to navigate. At some point, the idea changed to capturing it in the form of a book. As I began to compile, I committed to thirty new entries. When combined there were exactly seventy entries! So

I researched the number 70 and learned it was a number emphasizing spiritual awakening and enlightenment, inner-wisdom and understanding, discernment and thoughtfulness, endurance, and persistence of purpose. I decided to title the book 70 Days, 70 Ways: He Speaks to Me because each of the entries grew from an encounter with God whether big or small.

I just hope as you read this that something is deposited within you. I hope that however you experience God in your life that it will continue to be enhanced day by day and that you experience His glory. I hope that you are challenged to be your best self, forgiving of your worst self, and committed to constantly strive for greater. Keep your eyes open to see Him in places you might not have before, keep your ears open for His guidance and clarity, and keep your heart open to change.

Take 70 days and hear all the ways He speaks.

day 1.

KNOW YOUR PLACE

Luke 7:37-38

When a certain immoral woman from that city heard He was eating there she brought a beautiful alabaster jar filled with expensive perfume.

[38]Then she knelt behind him at his feet, weeping. Her tears fell on his feet, and she wiped them off with her hair. Then she kept kissing his feet and putting perfume on them.

Many things are unpredictable, but no matter the day of the week, three things are sure. One, the sun will rise. Two, the sun will set. Three, on some television network, you can find a reality television show. On the show, you will always find one castmate yelling at another about who is right and who is wrong. Often these conversations end with some version of "You better know your place!" I often find myself wondering what place they are referencing.

So, I embarked on a one-girl journey to see where my place would be. I was curious about how I would respond and what I would say if someone said those sorts of things to me. I had to be truthful with myself. I would probably end up calling on Jesus's name to avoid losing my mind and ending up on a crime show! So, instead, I thought "What can I do to avoid such things?" What would be a better way to handle myself if I was ever in such predicaments?

God answered me by saying, "Your place is in Me." I was then reminded of two familiar stories. In the book of Luke, the account tells the story of Jesus being anointed with expensive oils by a woman the city deemed as immoral. When she entered to serve, she used the best oils she had, combined with her tears, to clean His feet. One of the disciples was angry and considered it to be a waste. He was offended by the comfort in which the lady even approached Jesus because he saw her as less than worthy. He felt she was out of place.

The other story being pretty similar is when Christ washed the feet of His disciples. To teach them a lesson in service, He was willing to bow and take care of their needs.

We often come across people who are the same way. They either believe themselves to be too good to be approached, or they believed others to be so beneath them that they never even consider inclusion. If we were to truly pattern ourselves after Christ, we would not be afraid to indulge in the company of all people. We would even be willing to humble ourselves to servitude.

Our place should be at the feet of God. In this placement, we worship, we praise, we serve, and we pray. This placement also shares the perks of being right in God's reach. Close enough to be chastened and to be lifted. Close enough to be heard and to hear.

I know my place, and you cannot put me there because I am already here.

day 2.

DO YOU BELIEVE IN MAGIC?

Matthew 19:26

...with God all things are possible

Some things in life are timeless—their essence and "wow" factor never fading. Disney is a fan favorite with a very large following and plenty of timeless stories. It is known for being the land of magic and fairy tales. It tells the stories of people with troubled pasts, whose journeys bring them a prince, a kingdom, and a happily ever after. One familiar song by Disney says, "Tale as old as time, song as old as rhyme, beauty and the beast."

Another example of timelessness is the life of Christ. Whether you are a believer or not, you know the story of Jesus. You know He came, lived, died, and lives. You know the beauty of His sacrifice and how it redeems us from all our beastly transgressions. You know the classic rules of expectations; you know the timeless reward of choosing to believe. You know choosing to deny those rules also gains a timeless curse.

We all know the story, but do we all choose to believe?

God is the world's greatest magician. He is the Creator of all things by simply speaking them into existence. Some do not believe in magic, but faith has its similarities. The way faith makes something out of our nothing, it can change the impossible into the possible.

Just as a fairy godmother can come along and bippity boppity boo it for Disney princesses, God can do it for you. You see, the "magic" of God is just as amazing; we, too, have troubled pasts that God can declare forgiven. We, too, can have our very own prince (after all, Christ is the Son of our King). We, too, can inherit a kingdom where we are free to reign. We, too, can have a happily ever after. But once again, do you believe?

day 3.

WHILE YOU WERE OUT

1 Samuel 15:29

And he who is the Glory of Israel will not lie, nor will He change His mind, for He is not human that He should change His mind!

A lot can happen in a few hours, days, or weeks. You can plan with targeted goals of completion, start strong, hit a few marks, and somehow become distracted.

If you really want to become dedicated to something, it only takes three weeks to create a habit. Although true, sometimes no matter our efforts, we may slip back into old routines or lack dedication. "Checking out" is sometimes easier than dedication.

Right?

It made me think "What if God handled us the same way?" What if He did not stay true to His word and went back on His promises? What if God made a vow and began the declaration with zeal and determination, then slowly lost interest in our potential? Yikes.

That is a scary thought. I think of the times I have looked back and marveled at how consistent His mercy has been, even when I was not as faithful. We must be mindful not to treat God as a receptionist. Just because He takes note of our actions and supplies provisions for our needs, it does not mean He is our personal assistant. It is our job to be of service, not the other way around.

So today I ask you: How guilty are you of this from day to day? How frequently do you check out on your spiritual responsibility and hope the spirit will just take the message for you?

day 4.

LOYALTY, LOYALTY, LOYALTY

James 1:6-8

But when you ask Him, be sure that your faith is in God alone. Do not walver, for a person with divided loyalty is as unsettled as a wave of the sea that is blown and tossed by the wind.

⁷Such people should not expect to receive anything from the Lord.

⁸ Their loyalty is divided between God and the world, and they are unstable in everything they do.

For every command my brain gives, my subconscious gives at least two responses. One is always the loving benefit of the doubt; the other is the concrete wall of "you did it on purpose, and I know you did!"

The first of the two carries a certainty of hope. It subliminally promises me each situation has a silver lining. Despite how thin it may be and how impossible it may seem, I retain confidence it is there.

On the other hand, the second response is convinced malice could be uncovered in the situation. Therefore, it peeks around the corner of every memory and past experience and develops a verdict always ready to shout, "I told you so!"

Either way, we have to try to maintain focus. The goal is to train our brains to think Godly as much as possible. No time for anxiety or defensive thinking. Instead of judging a situation or assuming the worst, we have to learn to pause, pray, and await peace. Remember the battle is not yours; it is the Lord's.

day 5.

YOU'RE IN GOOD HANDS

Jeremiah 29:11

"For I know the plans I have for you," declares the Lord, "plans to prosper you and not to harm you, plans to give you hope and a future."

God has designed each of us with a purpose and a plan. The good news is the plan comes with assurance and not insurance. The not-so-good news is many of us have confused assurance with insurance.

Google defines insurance as an arrangement by which a company or government agency provides a guarantee of compensation for specified loss, damage, illness, or death in return for payment of a premium. While assurance is defined as a positive declaration—a promise—intended to give confidence.

Be honest. If you had to choose, which seems like the better deal, the one where compensation is contingent upon specifics in return for payment or the positive declaration which comes with a promise specifically from God?

We both know what the better deal is. Yet rather than trusting God's plan, we opt for the "Fickle Faith Protection Plan." In our worries, we disregard the God-given signs and turn left when we were right where He wanted us to be.

We must learn that while God's instructions may not be the quickest route, it is the route with the better view of your future, and it determines the magnitude of enjoyment once you get there. Trust His plan.

day 6.

COMPLETELY

Matthew 6:25-34

That is why I tell you not to worry about everyday life—whether you have enough food and drink, or enough clothes to wear. Isn't life more than food, and your body more than clothing?

²⁶Look at the birds. They don't plant or harvest or store food in barns, for your heavenly Father feeds them. And aren't you far more valuable to him than they are?

²⁷Can all your worries add a single moment to your life?

²⁸And why worry about your clothing? Look at the lilies of the field and how they grow. They don't work or make their clothing,

²⁹Yet Solomon in all his glory was not dressed as beautifully as they are.

³⁰And if God cares so wonderfully for wildflowers that are here today and thrown into the fire tomorrow, He will certainly care for you. Why do you have so little faith?

[31]So don't worry about these things, saying, "What will we eat? What will we drink? What will we wear?"

[32]These things dominate the thoughts of unbelievers, but your heavenly Father already knows all your needs.

[33]Seek the Kingdom of God above all else, and live righteously, and He will give you everything you need.

[34]So don't worry about tomorrow, for tomorrow will bring its own worries. Today's trouble is enough for today.

When you free your faith to work and train your trust to be unwavering, just sit back and watch God work!

It took me a while to learn this. I cannot honestly say I have perfected it, but I have come a very long way. I have been using a "peace word." While talking with a person very important to me, I was reminded I do not have as much control over situations as I would like to believe.

After speaking with her, I could no longer dare to say I trusted God to handle a situation and still check in on it every now and then. God expects us to let it go completely and trust Him with whatever we are wise enough to release. Therefore, when I have prayed about a situation and later find myself worrying, complaining, or feeling the urge to "peek" into my own weak abilities, my spirit reminds me with a small whisper "Completely."

It is funny how one second of reasonable thinking mellows out the insanity rumbling in your mind. Just like God spoke to Job in the storm and Jesus calmed the seas, your mountains, too, can be moved.

Are you willing to completely trust? Grant yourself the peace in knowing it is covered and well taken care of.

day 7.

OPEN DOORS

Revelations 3:7-8

Write this letter to the angel of the church in Philadelphia. This is the message from the one who is holy and true, the one who has the key of David. What He opens, no one can close; and what He closes, no one can open:

[8] I know all the things you do, and I have opened a door for you that no one can close. You have little strength, yet you obeyed My word and did not deny Me.

Imagine two large golden doors. What if these doors were a gateway to anything you have ever wanted, thought you needed, or for which you have diligently prayed? What if it was an escape from patterns you live in day to day? What if it paved a road directly to your biggest goal in life? What if it held the answers to all the questions of life puzzling you? What if it separated you from the people whose opinions are never constructive but tear you apart word by word? What if it held new chances and opportunities never given to you before? What if it stood right in front of you? Would you open it and walk in?

Would you have any reason to desire to return to where your feet stood before you decided to walk through those doors?

These doors represent all we can have by serving God and following Christ Jesus. All it takes is faith to step in and never look back. Once you do, your desires are given according to His will. Your needs are supplied before you even know you need them. You find peace in knowing that God hears, and He knows. Each day carries a new blessing, so repetitive, mundane patterns no longer exist. Goals are not only reached but surpassed. Wisdom gives insight to the things around you. People's opinions fall on deaf ears.

God opens door after door for those who trust Him enough to know that whatever lies on the other side, whether it be blissful times or blistering moments, He will carry you through.

Is your faith as golden as these doors?

day 8.

ARE YOU A TWO-CENT CHRISTIAN?

James 4:5-17

Do you think the Scriptures have no meaning? They say that God is passionate that the spirit he has placed within us should be faithful to him.

6And he gives grace generously. As the Scriptures say, "God opposes the proud but gives grace to the humble."

7So humble yourselves before God. Resist the devil, and he will flee from you.

8Come close to God, and God will come close to you. Wash your hands, you sinners; purify your hearts, for your loyalty is divided between God and the world.

9Let there be tears for what you have done. Let there be sorrow and deep grief. Let there be sadness instead of laughter, and gloom instead of joy.

¹⁰*Humble yourselves before the Lord, and He will lift you up in honor.*

¹¹*Don't speak evil against each other, dear brothers and sisters. If you criticize and judge each other, then you are criticizing and judging God's law. But your job is to obey the law, not to judge whether it applies to you.*

¹²*God alone, who gave the law, is the Judge. He alone has the power to save or to destroy. So, what right do you have to judge your neighbor?*

¹³*Look here, you who say, "Today or tomorrow we are going to a certain town and will stay there a year. We will do business there and make a profit."*

¹⁴*How do you know what your life will be like tomorrow? Your life is like the morning fog—it's here a little while, then it's gone.*

¹⁵*What you ought to say is, "If the Lord wants us to, we will live and do this or that."*
¹⁶*Otherwise you are boasting about your own pretentious plans, and all such boasting is evil.*

¹⁷*Remember, it is sin to know what you ought to do and then not do it.*

———————————————

Let me introduce you to my theory—the Two-Cent Christian Theory.

Many Christians are stuck at a two-cent praise level. A Two-Cent Christian is a Christian who has accepted Christ as their Savior, and to them that is enough. They use their salvation as a safety deposit. "As long as I am saved, I'll make it Into the kingdom of heaven."

Do not get me wrong; there is nothing wrong with being saved, but there is something wrong with being content with the minimum. Some people come to church Sunday after Sunday because it is habitual, but is the relationship real? Rather than focusing on the service, Two-Cents are more concerned about who is walking in, the clothes they are walking in, and the time they are walking in. Their focus is in the wrong place, which limits their praise.

God desires to use His people in many ways. Make yourself usable. When we praise and bless God, we will get blessed in return.

What is the next level, and how do you get there? A five-cent praise level. It is simple. A Five-Cent Christian shows growth. At this level, a Christian has begun to build a relationship and a stronger foundation with God. They pray more, they read the Word more, and they begin to stop stressing over minor things by letting God handle more issues. A Five-Cent Christian is not afraid of praise, but even then, is it enough? Our goal as Christians should always be to have the best relationship we can with God and to introduce others to Him as well.

So, what is the next level? A ten-cent praise level. When you become a Ten-Cent Christian, you have reached double numbers, symbolizing double effort. Not only are you not afraid of praise but you are not afraid of commitment. You become faithful to serving God's people, finding ways to build relationship with

Him. You may begin attending Sunday school, participating in prayer service, and Bible study. You become so thirsty for God you are willing to sacrifice time doing other things for time spent in His midst (presence). Growth in God is a blessing. To move to higher levels and to be covered in His favor is a sweet, sweet gift. It is totally worth the sacrifice. After all, He gave His best. Should you not do the same?

The final level opens a door to a copious number of blessings and favor. Although it is the last level, it is limitless. A twenty-five-cent praise level. It is the level where you humbly submit to God's requests, and He uses you to bless others. It is when the knowledge you have gained turns into Godly wisdom. You can boldly face trials because you know He would not place more on you than you can bear. My favorite part about this level is that once your twenty-five-cent piece combines with the trinity of God the Father, God the Son, and God the Holy Ghost, you are made whole in the fullness of what He desires you to be.

Why settle for the deposit? Take the time to know God the way He knows you. It is an investment that will never fail, and you will never regret it.

day 9.

ACCEPTING WHAT GOD ALLOWS

Job 36:22-29

*Look, God is all-powerful.
Who is a teacher like Him?*

*²³No one can tell Him what to do,
or say to Him, "You have done wrong."*

*²⁴Instead, glorify His mighty works,
singing songs of praise.*

*²⁵Everyone has seen these things,
though only from a distance.*

*²⁶Look, God is greater than we can understand.
His years cannot be counted.*

²⁷He draws up the water vapor

and then distills it into rain.

*²⁸The rain pours down from the clouds,
and everyone benefits.*

*²⁹Who can understand the spreading of the clouds
and the thunder that rolls forth from heaven?*

Accepting what God allows is easily said but not easily done. It is also easy to only see the things in our life when they are not what we want them to be. We see our struggles big and bold. So much so, it can cause us to question God. We wonder, "Why me?" or "Why this?" or "Why that?" while the whole time God is asking "Why doubt?"

Be reminded of Job, a man who served God relentlessly. Job had so much faith and great discipline that when Satan asked God for permission to test him, God knew he would stand firm in his faith. Job had not sinned against God. He was not deserving of his perils, but God allowed them to happen as an opportunity to teach Satan that great faith is unmovable.

Stripped of everything he owned and loved, Job still knew God to be true. Even when struck with illness, he knew God to be true. It was not until friends questioned Job and Job's faith that he began to question God as well. When he did, God greeted him with a fierceness.

God warned Job to brace himself like a man. These instructions were not to imply his strength as we would assume, but they were to remind him of his true aptitude in comparison to a god, our God.

God reminded Job of something that can be helpful to all of us to remember. We were not around when God created everything, therefore, it is not fair to question His design. We were not there when he crafted the world, so we cannot begin to understand how He grieves its demise. We were not there when He shielded us from harm, so we are sometimes unaware of the grace. We were not there when He commanded the morning, so we cannot command the events of a day nor how it ends. We are not God, we are not His equals, and we will never understand His wisdom and can never question His hands.

It leaves one choice: Accept what God allows.

Often, we allow our observations of other people's situations or their opinions of our own to pull us away from our faith. It is in these moments of doubt that sin truly creeps in. We begin to fear things we had not before, we begin to plan for destruction, or we accept a fate other than the one God intends for us. We become stagnant in our missions—not because God is not moving us but because we do not exercise unwavering faith. We begin to fail assigned tasks because we are stuck on minute details.

Even when it seems unnecessary or unfair, God has a plan. Despite the turmoil around you, blessings are still there as well. Even when you feel stripped of all things that matter to you most, you need to know God is still love and a double blessing is heading your way.

Change your prayer. No longer ask God "Why?" Ask Him "How?" "How can I make it through?" "How can I give You the glory in this?" "How can You use me even now?" "How can I praise Your name right here in the middle of my mess?"

Being a Job can be a full-time job, but its reward is fully worth it.

day 10.

QUICK QUESTION(S)

John 10:25-30

Jesus replied, "I have already told you, and you don't believe Me. The proof is the work I do in My Father's name.

26But you don't believe Me because you are not My sheep.

27My sheep listen to My voice; I know them, and they follow Me.

28I give them eternal life, and they will never perish. No one can snatch them away from Me,

29for My Father has given them to Me, and He is more powerful than anyone else.
Prophecy and speaking in unknown languages and special knowledge will become useless. But love will last forever!
No one can snatch them from the Father's hand.

bianca chandler

[30]"The Father and I are one."

Quick question…How does God's voice sound to you? Does it sound like peace and quiet? Does it sound like your favorite song? Does it sound like a sweet voice of guidance? Have you heard it before at all? The truth is God's voice may be different to each of us. And that is okay.

Time and time again, in the word of God, we see Him speak to His people—whether it is directly or through a situation, a storm, or another person. Whether you hear His call in the rolls of thunder or in the quiet of the night, hearken and say "Yes?"

Some people assume the process is pray, ask, and get immediate answers. When they do not hear or experience what they expect, they think God has not heard nor has He answered. But even God's silence speaks volumes. It can instruct you to be still and wait, or it can be a clue you have ventured too far and can no longer hear His call.

Which brings me to my next question: Once you hear God, then what? Do you move immediately? Do you stand in awe thinking "Did that just happen? Did He just answer me?" Do you pray again because you were too busy and too spiritually noisy to hear the memo?

The best way to learn how God speaks to you is to listen for Him in everything. Find His glory in each new day. Take time to appreciate the small things and praise Him in all things. Hearken your heart before you hearken your ear. Most importantly, when He speaks, you will know. There is nothing mistakable about being in the presence of God. When you experience Him, you will know...hold on to it and never let it go. Seek Him and His voice daily!

day 11.

WHISPER "WOW"

Matthew 25:23

The master said, "Well done, my good and faithful servant. You have been faithful in handling this small amount, so now I will give you many more responsibilities. Let's celebrate together!"

Do you ever just take a step back, look at your life, and whisper, "Wow"? If you have not done so lately, then maybe you should.

Sometimes it is so easy to look at all the things going wrong around us. It is far easier to see the complexities of life rather than the positives. Positive things are often taken for granted because they work so well in your favor. Favorable means comfortable, and comfortable can sometimes mean ignorable. For instance, when you go sofa shopping, it is important to find a sofa that is durable and that feels nice. Maybe for the first week or so, you will say "I sure did a great job picking that sofa. Look how well it complements the space. Oh, it feels so nice." About three weeks go by, and you plop down and move on.

The same thing can happen with the blessings and good in our lives. When the blessing is new, we want to share the testimony with everyone. We would even shout it from the mountaintops. But eventually, the same blessing God is allowing to remain as a constant in our lives becomes so familiar until we plop into it and move on.

So why are we guilty of it? Simple answer: it is because the "right" or "good" things keep you afloat while issues snag you and hold up your travels—but only if you allow them.

Let us pick up where we left off on our previous example. Not too long after purchasing your sofa, you go to visit a friend. Upon arriving, you learn she, too, has purchased a new sofa. But she did not stop there! She also purchased the matching adornments. Pillows and all! The rug matches the ottoman, the throw matches the drapes, and you can still smell the wood-stained finishing. You travel home with the utmost disgust towards your once proud purchase, and the sense of gratitude fades. You are snagged by comparison and envy. Little do you know the pillows are covering the holes. The rug is covering battered floors. The ottoman supports struggling feet. The drapes are meant to hide hypocritical windows, and the paint is covering the furniture's damaged foundation.

Your blessings might not seem to be the same as those around you, but they are yours! God gives you exactly what you need. Matthew 25: 23 shows the reward of being faithful over few things is gaining many more. You must show constant gratitude in all you are given if you expect growth or expansion. Sometimes our snags are necessary. They keep us still long enough to call out for help and be reminded that the adornments are not an inheritance.

Enjoy what you are given and whisper "Wow."

day 12.

HE IS WORKING

2 Timothy 2:21

If you keep yourself pure, you will be a special utensil for honorable use. Your life will be clean, and you will be ready for the Master to use you for every good work.

We all experience things differently. We feel differently. Encounter differently. Imagine differently. Express differently. We all come from different places. Those things are obvious, but they all come down to what we choose to absorb in our surroundings—whether we come from great beginnings or a great big mess.

God views us the same way. No matter what choices you have made in life that might have left you feeling rusted, you are never worthless. Inside of you, God has planted seeds that are full of life and potential, but you must place yourself in a location of expectancy. No matter where life lands you, what curb you fall to, or where someone leaves you after using you up, God always has a plan.

If we look at the type of people God used in the Bible, it is never the ones the world would expect. Moses was the son of a slave but was raised as a prince. David, a shepherd boy, grew into a king. Noah, thought to be a fool, became father of the new world. In all these instances, they may have felt like fish out of water. In situations where others expected them to fail or be defeated, they rose and conquered.

Never allow your environment to define you. Trust God's ability to transform what the world expects you to become and replace it with what He has destined for you to be. Remember, tragedy can translate to triumph—even when you are uncomfortable, He is working. When you feel beaten up and battered, He is still working. Even in your emptiest and most gruesome moments, God still sees a vessel.

day 13.

GET RIGHT OR GET LEFT

2 Chronicles 7:14-16

Then if my people who are called by my name will humble themselves and pray and seek my face and turn from their wicked ways, I will hear from heaven and will forgive their sins and restore their land.

[15]My eyes will be open and my ears attentive to every prayer made in this place.

[16]For I have chosen this Temple and set it apart to be holy—a place where my name will be honored forever. I will always watch over it, for it is dear to my heart.

If you knew anything about anything in the early 2000s, you knew that Ja Rule and Ashanti were the best things since sliced bread! No matter when you turned on your radio, plugged in your laptop to dial up the Internet, or held your CD player extra tight so it would not skip on the school bus, you were probably listening to "I'm not always there when you call, but I'm always on time," and

"I gave you my all, so baby be mine." Or maybe you were singing Usher's "Confessions."

Either way, there are some lessons to be learned from these songs. You know I love analogies, so let us tie it all together. God is never too far away. In fact, He is always there. When we call, He answers. Even if the answer is silence, there is still meaning.

When we committed to choosing God by following Christ, we committed to giving our all. We often fail to remember that wherever we go, we carry our spirit there as well. So, when we sin, whether it is our first mistake or the same mistake for the hundredth time, God is always there. There is always an opportunity to dust yourself off, try again, and confess what you have done.

God is very merciful and views us differently from how we deserve to be viewed. It is interesting how it works. As filthy and unworthy as we truly are, when He sees us, He does not see our sins but the blood of Jesus. Unfortunately, many of us have mistaken what this truly means. Let us not forget God is all knowing. Although mercy covers us, we should never assume God is not informed of our dirty deeds.

Jonathan Reynold's song "No Gray" follows the daily struggle of temptation versus righteousness. It depicts how God desires for us to make efforts to choose the right thing. The lyrics say "And no I'm not a fool, I know eventually I'm gonna have to choose. And, really I don't wanna lose my ticket into heaven and a chance to be used by You." Are you willing to risk your ticket in?

He has afforded us the chance to turn away from our wickedness and submit to Him. In 2 Chronicles 7:14, we are told that sincere repentance not only gives us forgiveness but restoration.

How beautiful it is to not only be forgiven but transformed.

day 14.

WHERE TO GO?

Proverbs 3:5-6

*Trust in the Lord with all your heart;
do not depend on your own understanding.*

*⁶Seek His will in all you do,
and He will show you which path to take.*

I once facilitated a session where I used the analogy of two familiar tools for navigation— a GPS to discover our Map.

For years, people have relied on maps to travel the world. Sometimes they can be a little hard to understand. There are lines all over the place, different colors to specify this and determine that, and sometimes it seems like the key is just about worthless. Unlike the shopping mall map, there is not a giant sign with a convenient star that reads "You are here." It is the exact opposite—not only do you have to discover where you are trying to go, but you must also locate where you are right now.

Now, let us look at a GPS. It is a far more complex tool than a map yet far simpler to use. You power up the device, turn on your location, type in the address and bam—it will get you there. The funny thing is while so many people now discredit maps or refuse to use them, they forget to acknowledge that the GPS uses the same map. It just puts you on a straighter path because it has more understanding about where you are and where you want to go.

As we travel through our Christian journey, if given the honor, God allows us to see a glimpse of His plan, which is better known as our meaning and purpose. However, it pulls us out of our comfort zone and into an area with which we are not quite as familiar. But not knowing where you are going does not mean you are completely lost. You must take advantage of your resources. Although there are many routes to a location, trying to do it on your own can detour you, take way longer than needed, or—worst-case scenario—send you in the wrong direction. Even though many roads may get you there, all are not the most ideal. But like always, God is the best and only resource to get you through. When you power up your signal and send a cry out to God, He locates you, meets you there, and guides you in your meaning and purpose. Suddenly, what was once confusion is now a lot clearer. Traffic can be a lot like our challenges in life.

Just because you have been delayed, it does not mean you have been denied. Efforts that seemed ineffective begin to show promise. Viewpoints that looked gloomy become scenic views. Keys that did not give answers now open doors. Roadblocks are removed. Construction zones only make your route more enjoyable in the end. It might not always be the quickest of routes, but you can bet it will be worth the ride.

day 15.

MAY THE ODDS BE EVER IN YOUR FAVOR

1 John 5:4-5

For every child of God defeats this evil world, and we achieve this victory through our faith.

[5] And who can win this battle against the world? Only those who believe that Jesus is the Son of God.

Faith is a tricky thing. Some might even consider it to be a gamble. It is like entering a casino; taking the seat at the head of the table, eyeing down every opponent there; and with the utmost confidence, placing your entire life's savings on red-1. That is absolutely daring and unheard of even. But with a closer look, it all makes sense.

As the wheel spins and the ball of possibilities bops from one place to the next, you lean in to see. The game is rigged, and you are sure to win it. Only one number is a winner—red-1. All signs point back to God's plan because His is the only way. Only one color saves—red. It is the blood of Jesus Christ. Placing all your hope and trust in God is exactly what faith is. It is knowing that no matter the odds, they will always be in your favor.

Things of this sort are not easy to accept or understand, especially when life throws you curve balls you never expect like financial troubles, sickness, or death. It is so important to understand that unexpected situations do not mean you have been deserted.

Some wonder, in the event of tragedy, how they are to believe in God. They wonder what kind of God would allow this to happen. They question if faith is wasted energy, if prayers are wasted words, and if hope is wasted emotion. I am reminded of the story of Job. He was stripped of everything he loved and still maintained a spirit of worship.

Sometimes we forget the contract. Our salvation is contingent upon our belief. Furthermore, it is contingent upon our belief that, regardless of the day or circumstance, God is still a God who saves. Even He suffered the loss of His beloved son as He saved us from damnation.

In some instances, we cannot see the blessings that surround us because we are counting the things we have lost. Yet just like Christ, and because of Him, things such as death do not have to mean forever. Even when God removes things from our lives, it is still with a purpose for the plan. Even when you do not understand, it is still in your favor.

When we put our faith in the Wheel, we may feel spun around, or anxiety may build about where it will land; but the odds will always be in our favor. The announcer has already blinked the lights and announced you as a winner, so collect your prize and thrive, baby, thrive!

day 16.

HOW DO YOU SEE IT?

1 Corinthians 3:1-9

Dear brothers and sisters, when I was with you, I couldn't talk to you as I would to spiritual people. I had to talk as though you belonged to this world or as though you were infants in Christ.

²I had to feed you with milk, not with solid food, because you weren't ready for anything stronger. And you still aren't ready,

³for you are still controlled by your sinful nature. You are jealous of one another and quarrel with each other. Doesn't that prove you are controlled by your sinful nature? Aren't you living like people of the world?

⁴When one of you says, "I am a follower of Paul," and another says, "I follow Apollos," aren't you acting just like people of the world?

⁵After all, who is Apollos? Who is Paul? We are only God's servants through whom you believed the Good News. Each of us did the work the

bianca chandler

Lord gave us.

⁶I planted the seed in your hearts, and Apollos watered it, but it was God who made it grow.

⁷It's not important who does the planting, or who does the watering. What's important is that God makes the seed grow.

⁸The one who plants and the one who waters work together with the same purpose. And both will be rewarded for their own hard work.

⁹For we are both God's workers. And you are God's field. You are God's building.

Perspective and perception matter far more than they are credited. We grow at different rates and see things from different heights. A crawling baby's view of the world is much different than a 5'10" adult's view. Likewise, the baby's perception of what is going on in its environment is completely different as well.

For imagination's sake, let us say you have booked a flight for a summer getaway. Check-in was flawless, your airline will be serving complimentary snacks, you were assigned the exit seat with the most leg room (placing you far enough away from the panicking first-time rider), your seat neighbor is a petite older woman, and it is obvious it is not her first rodeo; you are absolutely convinced it will be the best flight of your life. Then suddenly, a frazzled mother boards with an eight-month-old baby who is clearly traumatized and crying for all of heaven to hear. It becomes very apparent that not only you, but also other members, are disappointed to be on a flight with a crying baby. The passenger behind you says, "That child is screaming bloody murder."

Here is where perspective and perception matter. Do you become frustrated with the mother and her baby, demanding she regain control of her child? Or do you implement a caring spirit that understands everything going flawless for you upon arrival may have been ten times harder to do with a baby in hand? Do you show compassion and understand that while you are embarking on the thirty-second flight of your life, the baby has never heard these sounds, seen this many people, or experienced how cold are the TSA officer's hands despite being gloved?

Life is the same way. We are not aware of other people's experiences or how they see the world. We are not aware of what may be new or traumatic for them. Tests we may have encountered several times can be new to someone else. In those instances, our jobs should not be to judge but to extend tolerance and assistance if able. Just like babies, we all encounter things that push us beyond our comfort zones.

Babies' experiences are new to them, and their perception reflects as much. They begin to hear things they have never heard, they experience people differently, and they find a way to deal with the world's screening process. On the flip side, there are the people who have gained experiences and have grown accustomed to the screening and the expectation of occasional hiccups. They know how to jump on board, relax, and let the pilot have full control.

Although we may all be at different levels of understanding and our lines of sight may be a little different, no matter what your perception may be, always keep your perspective in check. Remember to be mindful of all people, taking the time to show an understanding and compassionate spirit.

So, ask yourself, on this flight of life, how do you see it?

day 17.

GROW UP

Hebrews 5:11-14

There is much more we would like to say about this, but it is difficult to explain, especially since you are spiritually dull and don't seem to listen.

¹²You have been believers so long now that you ought to be teaching others. Instead, you need someone to teach you again the basic things about God's word. You are like babies who need milk and cannot eat solid food.

¹³For someone who lives on milk is still an infant and doesn't know how to do what is right.

¹⁴Solid food is for those who are mature, who through training have the skill to recognize the difference between right and wrong.

_____

Many things in life come with a time stamp, which is evident well before we are even conscious of it. Upon conception, an automatic clock begins ticking. If everything works according to "plan," you have right at or a little over nine months to grow. From that point, you go through stages of growth. Your family cheers for you to crawl by a certain point, walk by a certain point, to be potty trained, develop social skills, to master algebra, finish high school, and achieve a degree. There are countless clocks set, expectations created, and visions of what you and others would like to see you become. And then there is God's clock—one that does not operate on our time.

It is not periodic. It does not measure minutes or seconds—but seasons and spiritual works. Just like physical life, God desires to see us grow spiritually. We cannot exist in His time and not expect change. We must be willing to move from comfort because it means growth. Often, we become satisfied in saying we are believers, but we are not actively seeking what God desires of us beyond that. An example would be a teenager who is capable of responsibility but still behaves as a young child. His or her behavior is not encouraged or tolerated. At that stage of development, they are expected to show some reflection of their age. Likewise, it is unreasonable behavior of a believer to say he or she believes and still behaves as a babe in Christ.

As we grow in the wisdom of God, we are expected to exemplify growth. We should be able to show love, compassion, joy, faith, and bear witness of who God is. As an unknown author said, "Our Christian journey is not about perfection but progression." To progress and grow in God's Word you must be willing to teach him. A child learns by example. The best example is set before us and detailed through the life of Jesus Christ. Nurture a relationship in which strong points are trust and communication. Find people in Christ who will cheer you on.

It is okay if you begin crawling because every person starts somewhere. Just do not crawl forever. Take joy in noticing your growth. Stand for Jesus, walk in His footsteps, chase behind Him, train your faith, speak to Him with confidence, master the troubling problems, finish what you start, and achieve the end goal.

day 18.

WHO YOU WIT?!

Luke 7:1-10

When Jesus had finished saying all this to the people, he returned to Capernaum.

²At that time the highly valued slave of a Roman officer was sick and near death.

³When the officer heard about Jesus, he sent some respected Jewish elders to ask him to come and heal his slave.

⁴So they earnestly begged Jesus to help the man. "If anyone deserves your help, he does," they said,

⁵"for he loves the Jewish people and even built a synagogue for us."

⁶So Jesus went with them. But just before they arrived at the house, the officer sent some friends to say, "Lord, don't trouble yourself by coming to my home, for I am not worthy of such an honor.

⁷I am not even worthy to come and meet you. Just say the word from where you are, and my servant will be healed.

⁸I know this because I am under the authority of my superior officers, and I have authority over my soldiers. I only need to say, 'Go,' and they go, or 'Come,' and they come. And if I say to my slaves, 'Do this,' they do it."

⁹When Jesus heard this, he was amazed. Turning to the crowd that was following him, he said, "I tell you; I haven't seen faith like this in all Israel!"

¹⁰And when the officer's friends returned to his house, they found the slave completely healed.

I am sure you have heard the saying "real recognizes real." There is a story in the gospel of Luke 7 in which a young Roman officer humbled himself enough to the authority of Christ to have faith and ask for His help. The story stands out in the Bible because Roman soldiers have been documented to be the most brutal soldiers in all of history. They were men who were powerful, respected, fearless, and viewed as the crème de la crème of their society. The officer impressed Christ because he was a man with power and an owner of many men; but he recognized Jesus's awesome power to heal and set free. In that moment, he was not concerned with his wealth or power—only with knowing neither of the two was enough to get him the results he wanted.

We live in a society where everyone feels the need to prove who they are. We have become so consumed with seeming independent and prosperous until we forget we could have so much more. Instead of functioning in the totality of our power and reaping all the blessings God has waiting for us, we try to do it alone. But know you can do all things through Christ who strengthens you. Be humble. Ask for strength and G-up (God-up, that is).

day 19.

TRUSTING IN TRIBULATION

Psalm 55

*Listen to my prayer, O God.
Do not ignore my cry for help!*

*²Please listen and answer me,
for I am overwhelmed by my troubles.*

*³My enemies shout at me,
making loud and wicked threats.
They bring trouble on me
and angrily hunt me down.*

*⁴My heart pounds in my chest.
The terror of death assaults me.*

*⁵Fear and trembling overwhelm me,
and I can't stop shaking.*

bianca chandler

⁶Oh, that I had wings like a dove;
then I would fly away and rest!

⁷I would fly far away
to the quiet of the wilderness.

Interlude

⁸How quickly I would escape—
far from this wild storm of hatred.

⁹Confuse them, Lord, and frustrate their plans,
for I see violence and conflict in the city.

¹⁰Its walls are patrolled day and night against invaders,
but the real danger is wickedness within the city.

¹¹Everything is falling apart;
threats and cheating are rampant in the streets.

¹²It is not an enemy who taunts me—
I could bear that.
It is not my foes who so arrogantly insult me—
I could have hidden from them.

¹³Instead, it is you—my equal,
my companion and close friend.

¹⁴What good fellowship we once enjoyed
as we walked together to the house of God.

¹⁵Let death stalk my enemies;
let the grave swallow them alive,
for evil makes its home within them.

¹⁶But I will call on God,

and the Lord will rescue me.

*[17]Morning, noon, and night
I cry out in my distress,
and the Lord hears my voice.*

*[18]He ransoms me and keeps me safe
from the battle waged against me,
though many still oppose me.*

*[19]God, who has ruled forever,
will hear me and humble them.*

Interlude

*For my enemies refuse to change their ways;
they do not fear God.*

*[20]As for my companion, he betrayed his friends;
he broke his promises.*

*[21]His words are as smooth as butter,
but in his heart is war.
His words are as soothing as lotion,
but underneath are daggers!*

*[22]Give your burdens to the Lord,
and He will take care of you.
He will not permit the godly to slip and fall.*

*[23]But you, O God, will send the wicked
down to the pit of destruction.
Murderers and liars will die young,
but I am trusting You to save me.*

How do you handle tribulation? How do you greet stressful situations? After the initial moment of panic, which seems to grab hold to you and stunt all other thoughts besides complaints and defeat, what do you do? Some people accept defeat, refusing to even try. Some resort to survival instincts, immediately jumping to action. There is a famous line in the 2009 movie Taken, which says, "But what I do have are a very particular set of skills. Skills I have acquired over a very long career." He spoke with confidence because he knew that of which he was capable. As a Christian, what skills are you sporting?

I have a long career in trusting God. It is a profession I have not yet mastered, but I am pretty good at the job. As a matter of fact, it is the most rewarding job I have ever had. I show up, turn in a report of current issues, and Boss Man does the rest of the work. The job requires only a few things on your résumé: frequent prayer and faith. That is it! And although it is the best job ever, it requires a lot of humility. It means being able to admit when you are tired. Admitting when you do not have a clue of which next steps are the right steps. Admitting the workload is too much to bear.

Psalms 55 is a beautiful passage of scripture in which a cry was made to God. The author begins by confessing weakness, and their need for God. They address people who scorn them, fear that overwhelms them, their desire to escape, but during it all, they also declare in verse 16, "But I will call on God, and the Lord will rescue me." Amid acknowledging all the trouble that surrounds him, he makes a choice on the job to let the Boss take control. Verse 22 is a familiar beauty which states, "Give [cast] your burdens to the Lord, and He will take care of you. He will not permit the godly to slip and fall." There is a blessing in releasing the burden.

One last analogy for the road. Just as a fisherman goes for a day at the lake, you must go to the Lord. As you stand next to a sea of faith, filled with blessings waiting to be claimed, you must stand flat foot and firm. You must have solid and rooted faith. You must know burdens can be bait if used correctly. The same thing you are holding on to, once you cast it into the sea of faith, God will grab hold of it and you, turning your situation into one that is a blessed one. Remember, you must throw it out to God to get it back. Let go, and let God.

day 20.

WHEN WISDOM IS A WOMAN

Proverbs 9:1-12

Wisdom has built her house;
she has carved its seven columns.

²She has prepared a great banquet,
mixed the wines and set the table.

³She has sent her servants to invite everyone to come.
She calls out from the heights overlooking the city.

⁴"Come in with me," she urges the simple.
To those who lack good judgment, she says,

⁵"Come, eat my food,
and drink the wine I have mixed.

⁶Leave your simple ways behind, and begin to live;

learn to use good judgment."

*⁷Anyone who rebukes a mocker will get an insult in return.
Anyone who corrects the wicked will get hurt.*

*⁸So don't bother correcting mockers;
they will only hate you.
But correct the wise,
and they will love you.*

*⁹Instruct the wise,
and they will be even wiser.
Teach the righteous,
and they will learn even more.*

*¹⁰Fear of the Lord is the foundation of wisdom.
Knowledge of the Holy One results in good judgment.*

*¹¹Wisdom will multiply your days
and add years to your life.*

*¹²If you become wise, you will be the one to benefit.
If you scorn wisdom, you will be the one to suffer.*

The beauty in reading the word of God is the random revelations. Proverbs is written so beautifully to shape perspective. It uses subtle analogies to make life's lessons easy to comprehend. In Proverbs, wisdom is described as a woman, essentially promising that nurturing it will produce benefits, while ignoring it will bring suffering.

Many of us want to know so much about every little thing but refute wisdom. We pray for clarity but ignore God's words. A commonly quoted scripture, 2 Timothy 2:15, reads, "Study to show thyself approved." The approval is regarding God revealing more to you bit by bit. You must not only desire wisdom but be willing to work for it. When you are wise—and not just smart—it makes a difference. It is a level of knowledge accompanied by protection and comfort. Remember, wisdom warns as you wade while smarts suggest as you stumble.

day 21.

ALL WE NEED IS LOVE

1 Corinthians 13

If I could speak all the languages of earth and of angels, but didn't love others, I would only be a noisy gong or a clanging cymbal.

²If I had the gift of prophecy, and if I understood all of God's secret plans and possessed all knowledge, and if I had such faith that I could move mountains, but didn't love others, I would be nothing.

³If I gave everything I have to the poor and even sacrificed my body, I could boast about it; but if I didn't love others, I would have gained nothing.

⁴Love is patient and kind. Love is not jealous or boastful or proud

⁵or rude. It does not demand its own way. It is not irritable, and it keeps no record of being wronged.

⁶It does not rejoice about injustice but rejoices whenever the truth wins out.

*⁷Love never gives up, never loses faith, is always hopeful, and endures through every circumstance.
become useless. But love will last forever!*

⁸Prophecy and speaking in unknown language and special knowledge will become useless. But love will last forever!

⁹Now our knowledge is partial and incomplete, and even the gift of prophecy reveals only part of the whole picture!

¹⁰But when the time of perfection comes, these partial things will become useless.

¹¹When I was a child, I spoke and thought and reasoned as a child. But when I grew up, I put away childish things.

¹²Now we see things imperfectly, like puzzling reflections in a mirror, but then we will see everything with perfect clarity. All that I know now is partial and incomplete, but then I will know everything completely, just as God now knows me completely.

¹³Three things will last forever—faith, hope, and love—and the greatest of these is love.

What do you do in moments of peril and adversity? How do you stand confidently in your beliefs when forced compromise seems to be the only option? How do you handle opposition and oppression? The answer is only four letters strong but holds infinite power. LOVE.

God confirms things in the oddest of ways. While traveling to Phoenix, Arizona the summer of 2016, we learned news of the tragic shooting of Alton Sterling in my hometown of Baton Rouge, Louisiana. In the hustle and bustle of the week, I did not get to work further on the post beyond the introductory paragraph. While on the trip, my boyfriend shared lyrics to a song he wrote— a song focused on power and love.

Because I had not yet addressed the situation of things going on in the past few weeks, I wanted to be sure that when I spoke, my words had a certain caliber of countenance. The previous Sunday morning, while dressing for church, I heard Dr. Jeremiah on television explaining the difference between worry and concern. He described worry as getting stuck and consumed in a problem while concern motivates the search for a solution. I began to ask myself where I fell on the scale. Moments later, while en route to church, I learned of the slain officers in my hometown as well. I knew then where I stood.

I pose the question again: What should be done in these moments when turmoil is all around you? Although the solution of love is simplistic to say, some may not find it easy to do. God tells us in His word that love means longsuffering, patience, forgiveness, encouragement, empowerment, and peace. It means caring for people who might not have what you have, look like you look, believe what you believe, or even share your opinion. But despite all those differences, you consistently offer your best self—a self who does not seek revenge but trusts God to persecute. A self who does not look down and belittle but understands all people are God's people. A self who stands with the bravery of Paul; the constant willingness of Moses; obedience like Abraham, faith like Shadrach, Meshach, and Abednego; and a prayer life like Daniel. In those cases, the mission was not easy; yet love made it possible. Paul's love for Christ prompted him to stand and speak even when it meant death. Moses's love prompted tolerance for a group of people who were stubborn and defiant. Abraham's love prompted the willingness to give up everything. Shadrach's, Meshach's, and Abednego's love prompted a faith that culminated in the ability to dance amid a heated situation—literally. And Daniel's love prompted consequences that would not stick.

Loving others in hard moments may not show immediate tangible outcomes, but God is still in control. God has the final say. All He has given us is because of grace, mercy, and love. This world is not our home, but while here in the midst of the mess as Christians, our focus should be displaying love in all ways, always.

day 22.

WHO'S TO BLAME?

Proverbs 19:1-8

*Better to be poor and honest
than to be dishonest and a fool.*

*²Enthusiasm without knowledge is no good;
haste makes mistakes.*

*³People ruin their lives by their own foolishness
and then are angry at the Lord.*

*⁴Wealth makes many "friends";
poverty drives them all away.*

*⁵A false witness will not go unpunished,
nor will a liar escape.*

⁶Many seek favors from a ruler;

everyone is the friend of a person who gives gifts!

*[7]The relatives of the poor despise them;
how much more will their friends avoid them!
Though the poor plead with them,
their friends are gone.*

*[8]To acquire wisdom is to love yourself;
people who cherish understanding will prosper.*

Two children are running through a store. Their mother warns them to stop but has exhausted every ounce of her energy. They race around the corner full speed. One staggers, the other trips, and the high pitch of glass breaking echoes through the store. Simultaneously, the children point at each other and shriek, "He did it!"

We too are those children running through life. Closely cutting corners, ignoring the warning signs, and exhausting the resources we have. We stagger. We fall. We damage things around us. We blame. Where does accountability come into play? Who is truly to blame, the doubter or the doubted?

We often rush through life and try our luck at things rather than enjoying the life designed for us. We can easily miss the beauty of our surroundings and fail to see their worth until it has already shattered at our feet. We usually rush for two reasons. Either we do not trust the process, or we are overly anxious to get to the result. Both of which show doubt in God's ability to provide. Philippians 4:6 says not to be anxious about anything!

In the moments when we rush or try to get ahead of the route planned for us, we can crash into situations that could have been enjoyable if approached correctly. When we move too quickly, we can miss a preoperational period. In doing so, when it is time to come face to face with a new level, we are not prepared. Why doubt and move at your own speed when God already has your map and arrival time figured out?

day 23.

A STARVING SPIRIT

Romans 10:9-13

If you openly declare that Jesus is Lord and believe in your heart that God raised him from the dead, you will be saved.

[10] For it is by believing in your heart that you are made right with God, and it is by openly declaring your faith that you are saved.

[11] As the Scriptures tell us, "Anyone who trusts in him will never be disgraced."

[12] Jew and Gentile are the same in this respect. They have the same Lord, who gives generously to all who call on him.

[13] For "Everyone who calls on the name of the Lord will be saved."

I heard something amazing one day: "You are a spirit in a human body." It spoke volumes to me because God gave me the analogy of a starving child.

God sees us as His children. We are old enough to exhibit some sort of independence but still young enough to need constant guidance. We need encouragement and affirmation. We need love, support, and instruction. Last but not least, we need food. Some people may consider these things to be less essential than the next, but all are vital. Even though all are essential, let us just focus on the one we all might agree to be the most important food.

It has been proven the best results of health are produced in a child who eats AT LEAST three meals a day—breakfast, lunch, and dinner. The meals should be colorful, nutritional, and it helps if the food tastes good. If we are knowledgeable of how important it is to feed our human bodies, then why do we not advocate for our spirits in the same way? When Jesus was in the wilderness and tested by Satan, He declared man does not live on bread alone but on every word that proceeds from the mouth of God. So, I ask you, what are you feeding your spirit?

If you stay up long enough at night, you will see a commercial fade in really slowly with music that immediately touches your soul. The camera slowly pans to a young child in a third-world country with tear-filled eyes, weakened legs, exposed ribs, and a caved-in stomach. The voice of the commentator explains that for just a few cents a day you can change the life of the child you see on the screen. You grieve before thinking about it for a moment. Then, you follow the conveniences of changing the channel.

What if I told you the commercial could be comparable to God speaking of your soul? God does not desire for us to have a starving spirit. We were not designed to be filled with sorrows. We were not designed to be weak. We were not designed to be empty. For just a few moments a day, you can change your spiritual life. but unlike the commercial, there is no convenience in turning away. God has given us a guide to follow to stay healthy within Him. Just as you live day to day, being sure to feed yourselves meals that keep you filled, fed, and happy, you also must feed your soul. Just as you have breakfast, lunch, and dinner, you should pray, study, and apply on a daily basis. Surround yourself with the colorful blessings God has waiting. Build on the strength you gain in following His word. Taste and see the Lord is good.

You are a spirit in a human body. It may mean you need the extra guidance, encouragement, affirmation, support, and instruction sometimes. Do not forget you have already been given all you need. It only requires a little effort, so call the number below and get started today:

1-800-Romans 10:9-13

day 24.

IT ALL MEANS NOTHING

Psalm 100

Shout with joy to the Lord, all the earth!

²Worship the Lord with gladness.
Come before Him, singing with joy.

³Acknowledge that the Lord is God!
He made us, and we are His.
We are His people, the sheep of His pasture.

⁴Enter His gates with thanksgiving;
go into His courts with praise.
Give thanks to Him and praise His name.

⁵For the Lord is good.
His unfailing love continues forever,

and His faithfulness continues to each generation.

Growing up in churches or being surrounded by many believers, you hear references to seasons. Some might say, "Step into your season," "It's just for a season," or "It's a season of favor." Regardless of what the season may be, it is a strategic plan designed by God Himself.

While having a conversation with a dear friend of mine, I listened as she recounted how she had been blessed to be removed from her current world's norms and placed into the center of her heart's desires. It is a sudden change of season and a whole new level. It could be the same for many of us as well. Being familiar with the Words of God is like having the master key to every door. The Bible incases instructions to show us how to ask and how to receive. It declares that if our desires are in accordance to God's will, our requests are ours to claim.

You will often hear people say, "God blesses and places us right where He wants us to be." In addition, our behavior in those placements determines our enjoyment. If you are at a place you consider to be stagnant, nine times out of ten, your praise is stagnated, too. Consequently, instead of honoring God's consistency and praising Him for sustaining you, you choose to think you are stuck; as a result, you will miserably await a change. If you are placed at a new level and your first thought is to proclaim how self-made you are, soon your enjoyment will turn to loneliness. If you are at a new level and you are too busy observing the level of the person next to you, your enjoyment will soon be experienced as envy. Now if at a new level you always give God glory, you will continuously be filled with joy. Praise God where you are placed, and trust in Him regardless of what your surroundings indicate.

Your surroundings mean nothing. It is what is hosted inside of you that shows up on the outside of you and changes your surroundings. People gripe and complain that their lives are crumbling beneath their feet. They scoff, asserting life does not come with a manual. They whine about how no one knows what they are going through or that no one understands. When the Word of God clearly states great faith is the foundation to all things being made new. It should be encouraging to think on how God knows you like no other because He created you special in HIS image.

You must equip yourself with God's Word so no matter your level, the devil, or your surroundings, you know how to turn to Him.

day 25.

GLORY STORY

Daniel 4:2-3

I want you all to know about the miraculous signs and wonders the Most-High God has performed for me.

³How great are His signs, how powerful His wonders! His kingdom will last forever, His rule through all generations.

It is easy to establish a habit. You wake up daily, hop out of bed, and start prepping for your day. Your mind wanders into the things you must accomplish before the day's end. You decide within moments which of those things are vital and what can be put off until the next day. You complete your routine, traveling to wherever your daily destination may be, and meanwhile, you forget to thank God for safely keeping you in your sleeping, in your waking, and for equipping you once more with the ability to continue life with a sense of normalcy.

In those moments of forgetfulness, His grace and mercy are still sufficient. It is the daily happenings we become accustomed to and forget to give God the glory... The minute an issue arises or a storm blows in so strong until we cannot see the end, it becomes easy to complain and wonder where His goodness lies. However, when He pulls you out, you have a story to tell. It becomes not just your story. It becomes a story He intends you to use to proclaim His glory. Your Glory Story.

Tell the story, giving God the glory of how He changed your pain or despair, your fear or defeat, your confusion or brokenness into a victory. No testimony exists without a test. If you are currently in a storm, just as Jesus spoke to the sea and calmed its waters, God can calm your storm. When it becomes peaceful again, instead of gloating in the survival, humble yourself in the midst of your rescue.

day 26.

AND LEAD US NOT…

James 4: 5-8

Do you think the Scriptures have no meaning? They say that God is passionate that the spirit He has placed within us should be faithful to Him.

⁶And He gives grace generously. As the Scriptures say,
"God opposes the proud
but gives grace to the humble."

⁷So humble yourselves before God. Resist the devil, and he will flee from you.

⁸Come close to God, and God will come close to you. Wash your hands, you sinners; purify your hearts, for your loyalty is divided between God and the world.

_____

"I generally avoid temptation unless I can't resist it." I stumbled across this quote and found it not only to be funny but true. Sometimes the hardest thing to do in your Christian walk is to stand before something that tempts you the most and walk away. Why is temptation such a challenge? What about it seems too intriguing to pass by? Why does it always seem to grab hold and refuse to let go until you give in?

When Jesus taught His disciples to pray, one of the last requests He made before ending the prayer was to avoid temptation. "Our Father in heaven, hallowed be Your name. Your kingdom come, Your will be done, on earth as it is in heaven. Give us this day our daily bread, and forgive us our debts, as we also have forgiven our debtors. And lead us not into temptation but deliver us from evil." This detail alone lets us know Jesus was aware it is not easy. Yet be reminded, in Philippians 4:13, it is possible.

The first step toward resisting temptation is acknowledging what tempts you. You must be honest enough with yourself to know what things can lead you to sin. In doing so, when faced with these things, you can also admit weakness and ask God for strength. Secondly, you must be wise enough to know when to ask. Before willingly sinning, there is always an opportunity to decide.

Temptation is like a well-tailored suit. It has been made to catch your interest and perfectly conform to you. In that crucial moment when you must decide, the "suit"—or sin—seems to speak to you and glow. But even tailor-made suits come at a price—although it is a perfect fit, it is still sold at the department of Guilt and

Shame. Therefore, you become all dressed up with nowhere to go.

Choosing otherwise opens doors to many more options—options leading to blessings, which can be viewed by others as adornments. A custom-made blessing not only fits you; it opens doors for you. Every place you go, you are draped in the grace and mercy of God. Choosing God's way might not be easy, though, it definitely has the best rewards.

day 27.

MEEK ISN'T WEAK, HUMBLE DOESN'T GRUMBLE

Matthew 5:3-12

God blesses those who are poor and realize their need for him,
for the Kingdom of Heaven is theirs.

⁴God blesses those who mourn,
for they will be comforted.

⁵God blesses those who are humble,
for they will inherit the whole earth.

⁶God blesses those who hunger and thirst for justice,
for they will be satisfied.

⁷God blesses those who are merciful,
for they will be shown mercy.

*⁸God blesses those whose hearts are pure,
for they will see God.*

*⁹God blesses those who work for peace,
for they will be called the children of God.*

*¹⁰God blesses those who are persecuted for doing right,
for the Kingdom of Heaven is theirs.*

¹¹"God blesses you when people mock you and persecute you and lie about you and say all sorts of evil things against you because you are my followers.

¹²Be happy about it! Be very glad! For a great reward awaits you in heaven. And remember, the ancient prophets were persecuted in the same way.

Tale as old as time, song as old as rhyme...beauty and the beast. In life, you come across different types of people on a daily basis. There are people who are beastly: rude, impatient, and disgusted with everyone and everything. And there are those who are the opposite. They are beautifully kind, long-suffering, and find delight in small or all things.

There are stereotypes that accompany these behaviors. For instance, individuals deemed as beastly are not to be tampered with. Their rage somehow grants respect. Although the "respect" may be the consequence of an attempt at avoidance, people still try to stay on those individuals' nice side. Whereas people who are nice and patient seem to always be the person steadily tested or taken advantage of. Why is that?

There is a common saying: "kindness is taken for weakness." Somehow, over a course of time, people have associated a lack of aggression with being a pushover. Their choice of choosing peace and calmness equates to someone as not having the courage or knowhow to stand up for themselves, which is not the case.

Meekness and humbleness are both a choice as well as a lifestyle. It is the choice to elevate others, to exhibit compassion, extend forgiveness, refuse spite, dismiss anger, and push others towards doing the same. As Christians, we should make daily efforts to live by these measures. Remember, despite what others might think or believe, meek isn't weak, and humble doesn't grumble.

day 28.

MIRROR POWER

Romans 12:2-4

Don't copy the behavior and customs of this world, but let God transform you into a new person by changing the way you think. Then you will learn to know God's will for you, which is good and pleasing and perfect.

³Because of the privilege and authority God has given me, I give each of you this warning: Don't think you are better than you really are. Be honest in your evaluation of yourselves, measuring yourselves by the faith God has given us.

⁴Just as our bodies have many parts and each part has a special function, ⁵ so it is with Christ's body. We are many parts of one body, and we all belong to each other.

I find more recently my brain seems to be busier than ever. I dart from idea to idea, finding inspiration in all things, and I have been enjoying the little things.

Amid my creative excitement, Google Keep is an amazing app that keeps track of all the spontaneity going on in my mind.

One of the trends I notice in my notes to myself is to take time to learn me. It may seem cliché, but it is so important. You must know your likes and dislikes, your goals and checkpoints, your standards and expectations, your yes's and no's. You must be bold in who you are. It also means knowing where you are weak or what things make you vulnerable.

I lead a weekly peer-based Bible study. We have real conversations, discuss the challenges we face, and support each other through prayer and scripture. One principle we stand on is transparency. There is a definite burden in perfection and a guilt in hiding things. So, we practice being honest with ourselves and others. In doing so, it forces you to be clear with yourself and identify some things you might have looked past. Sometimes when we bury attributes, past hurts, or even secrets from other people, we hide them from ourselves. In doing so, we alter what our true depths should be by the contamination of dishonesty or denial. Realizing and acknowledging these things is when our true circumstance changes.

There is power in visibility. If you are bold in who you are, people should see a clear and definite you. If you do not quite have it figured out yet, the best start is always to look within.

day 29.

WHAT DOES YOUR HEART ASK FOR?

Psalm 37:4-6

*Take delight in the Lord,
and He will give you your heart's desires.*

*[5] Commit everything you do to the Lord.
Trust Him, and He will help you.*

*[6] He will make your innocence radiate like the dawn,
and the justice of your cause will shine like the noonday sun.*

Honesty is a great characteristic to have. Although, when it is time for me to be honest with others regarding religion, I take the extra step to be mindful of how I deliver the truth. If the goal is for the listener to be receptive, what I am saying cannot sound judge-y. It cannot sound like ridicule. It cannot sound like I have been gawking at their life's decisions, waiting for a chance to speak. So how to handle that?

I usually pray and ask God to lead my wording and to make my intent clear—to give whomever I am speaking with a heart that is willing to receive what I am going to say. Lastly, I pray for God to show me a message in the words. As Paul stated, by no means have I assumed I have arrived at any level of perfection. Each time I part my lips to minister to anyone, I open my heart for what God must tell me as well.

People love the scripture that reads, "God will grant the desires of your heart," but they skip the part that reads "to delight in Him." His own will does not mean whatever the "it" is you want so desperately will end in your happiness. "It" may just be a part of the course for you to learn God has ultimate control. Just because your desire seems like everything you want does not mean it is everything God has for you. But what is sure is God's will *will* be done.

Yes, again, it means sometimes the desires of your heart will be granted, but it will not end up the way you wanted it to. You must be strong enough in your faith to accept that He may give you exactly what you want ultimately for Him to give you exactly what you need!

I know it is a tough concept to accept. Having a relationship with God gives you the peace you want, need, and deserve—peace to know even though the moments or situations seem sucky, we do not serve a sucky God. It means knowing the moments we experience are just that—moments. They are the moments that come right before the best moments of your life. There is a portion of scripture instructing you to delight yourself in Him. Find joy in God.

He is a great God with so many plans for us. Sometimes it takes us longer to get where He desires us to be. The same "great God" is so great He grants our prayers. Occasionally, the things we want to "enjoy and cling to" so much we pray for them may be the very things sending us down a course that pulls us further from the road He has built where so much joy is waiting.
So, what to pray for?

Pray your desires become what God desires for you. Pray you acknowledge trials as learning opportunities and not as personal attacks. Pray for a heart that seeks God, enjoys what is given, delights in fellowship, and praises unconditionally. In this way, when He grants you your desires according to His will, it will be so in-tune until it rings the melodies of your praise.

day 30.

CONSTANT CONTENTMENT

Philippians 4:10-14

How I praise the Lord that you are concerned about me again. I know you have always been concerned for me, but you didn't have the chance to help me.

[11]Not that I was ever in need, for I have learned how to be content with whatever I have.

[12]I know how to live on almost nothing or with everything. I have learned the secret of living in every situation, whether it is with a full stomach or empty, with plenty or little.

[13]For I can do everything through Christ, who gives me strength.

[14]Even so, you have done well to share with me in my present difficulty.

The fourth chapter of Philippians is a wonder. It is filled with gratitude and a reminder to stay steadfast and focused on spreading the good news. It is a challenge to not worry about anything but to pray about everything. The scripture prompts us to rejoice always. It is an assurance of strength and an urge to be content in all things, encouraging believers to have joy in any and every situation.

To do so also means knowing the difference between happiness and joy. Happiness is temporary. It is contingent upon feelings and emotions. Whereas joy is spirit made and should be sourced from constant praise and gratitude.

People seem to be able to comply with most of these things but become a little hesitant at the "contentment" portion.

Why? Contentment is usually paired with a negative connotation. Rather than being seen as peaceful happiness and satisfaction, it is confused for complacency.

However, contentment is not complacency. It is not agreeing to settle for just anything. It does not mean adapting to an attitude that says "It is what it is." It does not mean accepting where you are and deeming yourself stuck. It means none of those things. Instead, it means trusting where God has placed you is intentional. Therefore, there is no need to worry or rush.

Contentment requires you to know that where you are and with what you have are enough. Because where God places, He provides. And where He assigns, He equips. And what He has designed, He manifests. And where He declares redeemed, He glorifies. Even when you do not understand His plan, it is already working. Even when it is not easy, remember it is not a permanent placement. It is only a portion of your process. So, rejoice now; you are to be elevated where He desires for you to go. As Paul stated, it is the secret to living in every situation.

day 31.

LOCKED AND LOADED

Malachi 3:8-12

"Should people cheat God? Yet you have cheated me!
"But you ask, 'What do you mean? When did we ever cheat you?'
"You have cheated me of the tithes and offerings due to me.

⁹You are under a curse, for your whole nation has been cheating me.

¹⁰Bring all the tithes into the storehouse so there will be enough food in my Temple. If you do," says the Lord of Heaven's Armies, "I will open the windows
of heaven for you. I will pour out a blessing so great you won't have enough room to take it in! Try it! Put me to the test!

¹¹Your crops will be abundant, for I will guard them from insects and disease. Your grapes will not fall from the vine before they are ripe," says the Lord of Heaven's Armies.

[12]*"Then all nations will call you blessed, for your land will be such a delight," says the Lord of Heaven's Armies.*

Some people say being a Christian requires too much; but actually, it requires only a few key things. As mentioned in a prior post, it calls for frequent communication with God, faith, loving others, forgiveness, and obedience. If the truth be told, that is not too much to ask; it just requires true dedication and actively choosing to do these things.

For some, talking to God seems inessential. They believe God's responses to be slow or their voice to be unheard, or they become frustrated with the answers God provides. But making that choice to talk to God establishes a relationship with Him, and it is good to be a companion of the King. For some, exemplifying faith seems to be just as pointless. They hope for certain outcomes and when it does not pan out the way they anticipated, rather than trusting God's plan, they resort to blame and pity. For some, loving others is not an option at all. They feel as if extending love to everyone is both unwarranted and impossible when it is as simple as making a choice to be Godly—choosing to forgive and to love anyway. After all, Jesus's sacrifice was unmerited. For some, obedience is boring. They believe sacrificing and giving God a portion of what He has so fairly requested is unreasonable but that small sacrifice opens doors like never before.

"What God has for me, it is for me," is a common saying and how beautiful to know it is true. Malachi 3:10 reads, "'Bring the whole tithe into the storehouse, that there may be food in my house. Test me in this,' says the Lord Almighty, 'and see if I will not throw open the floodgates of heaven and pour out so much blessing that there will not be room enough to store it.'"

Much like your home, when you need more space, you purchase a storage unit. If need be or if the possessions are really valuable, you pay the extra funds for a nice unit—one that is climate-controlled and secured.

God is the same way. When He pours out an abundance of blessings, although you might not be able to store it, what is for you, is for you. God has a climate-controlled storage with your precious blessings waiting in it. Even those things of which you are not even yet aware. It means whether you are in a warm season of your life or a cold season, God has you covered. No matter if the sun is shining or storm winds are blowing, your blessings are still yours and waiting. It means no one else has access to what God has set aside for you but you. It cannot be claimed, stolen, or put up for debate because God has sealed it just for you. It is yours to claim, but you must use your keys! Have keys that are just as strong!

A strong relationship with God in which you are able to trust the contract. Strong faith that even when the rain is pouring, you know all is well. Strong love that even persecution cannot deter. Strong forgiveness to greet individuals who may try you. And strong obedience with a heart that declares, "yes God." Remember, it is yours to claim!

day 32.

CHAOS

John 14:27-29

"I am leaving you with a gift—peace of mind and heart. And the peace I give is a gift the world cannot give. So, don't be troubled or afraid.

²⁸Remember what I told you: I am going away, but I will come back to you again. If you really loved me, you would be happy that I am going to the Father, who is greater than I am.

²⁹I have told you these things before they happen so that when they do happen, you will believe.

Week after week, there are new tensions that reach new heights in our communities, country, and news feeds. If the truth be told, our opinions got us to this point. But mostly I remain quiet because I have been observing and praying.

We are living in a time where everyone has so much to say but no time to listen. They have the boldness to critique and belittle but no courage to uplift and aid the ones who are in need. People are very willing to destroy and uproot families but are neglecting the opportunity to plant seeds of change. We see, on a daily basis, a contamination of minds with hate and confusion—where passionate origins are skewed to be disrespect. There are people who yell the laws of oppression but fail to live by the law of God, which is simply to love.

Love frees us from so many chains whether they be societal, systematic, environmental, or cultural. Unfortunately, we are not all linked to the chain of love but, consequently, are all trapped in the binds of chaos.

day 33.

SO GLAD

Psalm 95:1-7

*Come, let us sing to the Lord!
Let us shout joyfully to the Rock of our salvation.*

*²Let us come to him with thanksgiving.
Let us sing psalms of praise to him.*

*³For the Lord is a great God,
a great King above all gods.*

*⁴He holds in his hands the depths of the earth
and the mightiest mountains.*

*⁵The sea belongs to him, for he made it.
His hands formed the dry land, too.*

⁶Come, let us worship and bow down.

bianca chandler

Let us kneel before the Lord our maker,

[7] for he is our God.
We are the people he watches over,
the flock under his care.

Do you ever find yourself wagging your finger at God? Whoa there! Before you assume I have completely lost my mind, I do not mean wagging in disapproval—more like, "Ah, big guy, I see what you did there." Time after time He creates opportunities to minister to others through my own experience or through recycling the same inspiration someone else spoke into my life. How reassuring to know we have a God who hears our deepest woes and sends just what we need (or who we need) just when we need it most. I am so grateful for His listening ear and provisional hand.

day 34.

A QUICK REMINDER

Psalm 139

*O Lord, you have examined my heart
and know everything about me.*

*²You know when I sit down or stand up.
You know my thoughts even when I'm far away.*

*³You see me when I travel
and when I rest at home.
You know everything I do.*

*⁴You know what I am going to say
even before I say it, Lord.*

*⁵You go before me and follow me.
You place your hand of blessing on my head.*

bianca chandler

*⁶Such knowledge is too wonderful for me,
too great for me to understand!*

*⁷I can never escape from your Spirit!
I can never get away from your presence!*

*⁸If I go up to heaven, you are there;
if I go down to the grave, you are there.*

*⁹If I ride the wings of the morning,
if I dwell by the farthest oceans,*

*¹⁰even there your hand will guide me,
and your strength will support me.*

*¹¹I could ask the darkness to hide me
and the light around me to become night—*

*¹²but even in darkness I cannot hide from you.
To you the night shines as bright as day.
Darkness and light are the same to you.*

*¹³You made all the delicate, inner parts of my body
and knit me together in my mother's womb.
¹⁴Thank you for making me so wonderfully complex!
Your workmanship is marvelous—how well I know it.*

*¹⁵You watched me as I was being formed in utter seclusion,
as I was woven together in the dark of the womb.*

*¹⁶You saw me before I was born.
Every day of my life was recorded in your book.
Every moment was laid out
before a single day had passed.*

*17 How precious are your thoughts about me, O God.
They cannot be numbered!*

*18 I can't even count them;
they outnumber the grains of sand!
And when I wake up,
you are still with me!*

*19 O God, if only you would destroy the wicked!
Get out of my life, you murderers!*

*20 They blaspheme you;
your enemies misuse your name.*

*21 O Lord, shouldn't I hate those who hate you?
Shouldn't I despise those who oppose you?*

*22 Yes, I hate them with total hatred,
for your enemies are my enemies.*

*23 Search me, O God, and know my heart;
test me and know my anxious thoughts.*

*24 Point out anything in me that offends you,
and lead me along the path of everlasting life.*

Regardless of your now, God is your forever. Do not allow momentary emotions that are attached to extended memories affect your now and your tomorrow. We all go through troubling times in life. They leave us in what seems to be the pits of despair.

But remember Psalm 139! No matter where you go, whether it is your lowest moments or your highest, God knows and is there.

day 35.

TEARS

Psalm 126:4-6

*Restore our fortunes, Lord,
as streams renew the desert.*

*⁵Those who plant in tears
will harvest with shouts of joy.*

*⁶They weep as they go to plant their seed,
but they sing as they return with the harvest.*

I was once speaking with a friend, and before we knew it, we were sharing stories and tears. We joked about how often we cry together. I am sure you too have had a moment like this. There is a certain level of comfort in releasing and being vulnerable with each other. Later while talking, she mentioned wanting to get to the point of not having to cry over certain things. Although that is a fair thought to aspire to, we must remember our tears have purpose. Although they commonly accompany tough experiences in our lives, tears are not without reason.

Sometimes the world leads us to believe tears are a sign of weakness or defeat, which is so far from the truth. Tears are responses to experiences and small reminders of our presence in those moments.

Furthermore, every experience in life is a seed. As it roots, it becomes a memory or something that sticks with you. It becomes a part of you. So even the moments that are rooted in pain or heartache, they are planted. But there is a scripture which reads, "Those who plant in tears, will harvest with shouts of joy" meaning even though you cry over those things, regardless of how many times you cry or how hard you cry, you still grow. Inevitably, it becomes something you can eventually harvest and rejoice about.

I used to think bad things in life grew as weeds—just consuming and destroying every other thing around them. I have since learned differently. To have a harvest means there must be something to collect—meaning all is not lost. The hurt produces the tears, and each time you cry about it you release and heal a little. Regardless of how long the process may take, no part of it is a waste.

Your tears will turn around!

day 36.

BEING THE BEST YOU

Philippians 3:12-16

I don't mean to say that I have already achieved these things or that I have already reached perfection. But I press on to possess that perfection for which Christ Jesus first possessed me.

¹³No, dear brothers and sisters, I have not achieved it, but I focus on this one thing: Forgetting the past and looking forward to what lies ahead,

¹⁴I press on to reach the end of the race and receive the heavenly prize for which God, through Christ Jesus, is calling us.

¹⁵Let all who are spiritually mature agree on these things. If you disagree on some point, I believe God will make it plain to you.

¹⁶But we must hold on to the progress we have already made.

A huge part of my platform is teaching the concept of "Being Your Best Self" and what it means. It means to be honest and admit that in this moment, right where you stand today, that you might not have it all together. And that is okay. But it also means working your hardest to ensure that each day is a new effort and a new commitment to try.

I have tried to introduce this concept to my students in several ways. I have been willing to be open and transparent about myself, relying heavily on relationship building through sharing a bit of who I am by way of bomb stories in exchange for their complete attention. I realize I do not have much of their time; therefore, I am cautious to maximize the moments I do have. We have been covering topics from meaning and purpose, self-discovery, effective communication, conflict resolution, personal brand, and integrity.

We hope to be able to say we have a good handle on all those things. Regardless of age, gender, or creed, we all can stand to work in these areas a bit more. Commit the effort to not only yourself but to the people around you who interact with you daily. We all contribute to the world bit by bit, day by day. Believe you are deserving, equipped, and qualified! What part of you are you giving the world today?

day 37.

EVEN WHEN YOU DON'T KNOW WHY

Jeremiah 29:11-14

For I know the plans I have for you," says the Lord. "They are plans for good and not for disaster, to give you a future and a hope.

¹²In those days when you pray, I will listen.

¹³If you look for me wholeheartedly, you will find me.

¹⁴I will be found by you," says the Lord. "I will end your captivity and restore your fortunes. I will gather you out of the nations where I sent you and will bring you home again to your own land."

———————————————

Sometimes when God brings us to new levels, we miss an

opportunity of additional praise. Of course, we rejoice in the newness of the blessing. Of course, we bow in gratitude. Of course, we say, "thank you." But do not forget to reflect on the steps that got you where you are. In doing so, you can see the moments in which you felt abandoned, lost, or discouraged were essential in your next steps. It becomes inadmissibly evident that God never left your side. Even when it was awkward or you were not sure of why you were where you were, God had it all under control.

day 38.

MAKE IT COUNT!

Isaiah 40:28-31

Have you never heard?
Have you never understood?
The Lord is the everlasting God,
the Creator of all the earth.
He never grows weak or weary.
No one can measure the depths of his understanding.

[29]He gives power to the weak
and strength to the powerless.

[30]Even youths will become weak and tired,
and young men will fall in exhaustion.

[31]But those who trust in the Lord will find new strength.
They will soar high on wings like eagles.
They will run and not grow weary.

bianca chandler

They will walk and not faint.

What motivates you? What excites you? What gives you your spark? What aspects of yourself do you wish to modify? If able, what opportunities would you explore? What risks would you take? What is stopping you? Make today the day you change it all. Run harder behind your dreams. Feed your interest. Educate yourself. Fine-tune your work. Promote your passion. You get one life; make it count!

day 39.

BE GREAT!

Genesis 12:1-3

The Lord had said to Abram, "Leave your native country, your relatives, and your father's family, and go to the land that I will show you.

²I will make you into a great nation. I will bless you and make you famous, and you will be a blessing to others.

³I will bless those who bless you and curse those who treat you with contempt. All the families on earth will be blessed through you."

Motivation comes in many different variations. Sometimes it can be your positioning. Sometimes it can be your perspective. Sometimes it can be a breach of pattern. Sometimes it can be people. And sometimes it can be because you are pass furious. Regardless of what gets you there, cling to it and keep going.

Becoming comfortable is an achievement as well as a curse. Comfort implies that your current placement provides some level of physical ease and relaxation. Kudos to you. Kudos because you have either walked into a level of favor, or something you have done has allowed you to enjoy this comfort. Take heed; comfort can be dangerous.

Pope Benedict XVI said, "The world promises you comfort, but you were not made for comfort. You were made for greatness." What a thought! Sometimes we become complacent (as I have written about before), which halts us from continuing towards the more remarkable versions of our self.

Dig deep. Remember who you are and why you are. Not sure of the who or why? Ask God for answers that not only give guidance but that give you a jolt to run forward. Be great!

day 40.

RISE UP

Acts 3:1-11

Peter and John went to the Temple one afternoon to take part in the three o'clock prayer service.

²As they approached the Temple, a man lame from birth was being carried in. Each day he was put beside the Temple gate, the one called the Beautiful Gate, so he could beg from the people going into the Temple.

³When he saw Peter and John about to enter, he asked them for some money.

⁴Peter and John looked at him intently, and Peter said, "Look at us!"

⁵The lame man looked at them eagerly, expecting some money.

⁶But Peter said, "I don't have any silver or gold for you. But I'll give you what I have. In the name of Jesus Christ, the Nazarene get up and walk!"

⁷Then Peter took the lame man by the right hand and helped him up. And as he did, the man's feet and ankles were instantly healed and strengthened.

⁸He jumped up, stood on his feet, and began to walk! Then, walking, leaping, and praising God, he went into the Temple with them.

⁹All the people saw him walking and heard him praising God.

¹⁰When they realized he was the lame beggar they had seen so often at the Beautiful Gate; they were absolutely astounded!

¹¹They all rushed out in amazement to Solomon's Colonnade, where the man was holding tightly to Peter and John.

Are you making use of your authority?

Every believer has been equipped with the power to call things that are not as though they are. Do you make use of this power given to you?

In life, we have opportunities to change our situations or the situations of others around us. Often, we miss the opportunity to do so because we are not aware of the power residing within us. Just as Peter and John asked the man at the gates of Beautiful to rise, God is asking us to do the same thing. We are to stand and walk in the glory of the Lord. We have been challenged to a great task of spreading the gospel and recruiting new souls.

Before Peter and John were able to operate in their authority, they observed Jesus implement His. You must walk and talk with Jesus, study His word, know how God loves and provides, and you can do the same. Remember, you cannot proclaim what you do not know.

Once you have claimed your authority as yours, you, too, can speak to things and demand a change. We must be willing to gain the attention of others by speaking boldly to people and through people. You must speak through their hurts, their experiences, their falsehoods, their betrayals, and right to the soul. Assist in breaking the patterns of them pleading with the world for handouts and sufficiency and offer them a new freedom that grants the ability to run, leap, and shout.
Rise to raise others.

day 41.

BUT HOW TO DO IT?

Ephesians 4:31-32

Get rid of all bitterness, rage, anger, harsh words, and slander, as well as all types of evil behavior.

[32]Instead, be kind to each other, tenderhearted, forgiving one another, just as God through Christ has forgiven you.

Each week, I teach a Sunday school and a youth Bible study at my church. During one of the lessons, I was asked a familiar question: "How to forgive people?" After asking the question, before I could even attempt to respond, my student added a component, which foretold the quality of the answer she was expecting: "And I know God forgave us, and it's the right thing to do… but how?"

And it made me think. Often, we do things based on the principle of it being the right thing to do. But I challenge you today. Are you really doing it or going through the motions? I do not know a person in this world who has not been wronged, offended, or scared from an instance in life. Some people know the hurt you have experienced and choose to ignore it. Some people are spurred to act. Most people will advise you to just "forgive and forget." Many of us have understood forgiveness to be a task that remains ours after completion rather than truly checking it off the list. But just as my student asked, "How?"

In the moment, it was as if God whispered to me how to give her an answer to bring peace to not only her but so many of us as well. Stick with me here.

I like to use the definition of words leveraged with other knowledge to elaborate as I teach. God instructed me to find the definition of "for-" (not in the traditional sense of belonging but as a prefix). Dictionary.com defines it as: 1. a prefix meaning "away," "off," "to the uttermost," "extremely," "wrongly," or "imparting a negative or privative force."

And it defines "give" as a free transfer of the possession of (something) to (someone); hand over to.

So, "for," in this context, is negative and can be representative of whatever event or challenge is requiring you to "let go" and transfer the possession of the hurt. And it is not easy.

Meanwhile the Bible tells us in 2 Corinthians 9:6-7 that God loves a cheerful giver.

So here we are with a combination word—the prefix carrying a negative connotation and the suffix carrying a joyful expectation. Funny, right? It made me think of a battery. How, although the negative and the positive are complete opposites, once they are combined and placed in the hollowest setup, it works, and purpose comes to life.

It brings us to the first step of forgiveness, which is acknowledging it is hard.

Secondly, you must know not only is it hard but it is a daily decision. Just as a battery must connect to a circuit, so do we, which brings me to the final step of forgiveness.

We must draw from the circuit of love. It creates the charge that motivates the why. Google defines circuit as a roughly circular line, route, or movement that starts and finishes at the same place. Everything starts and ends with love. The hurt we experience is the rough middle.

No one is telling you that forgiveness must happen right now in this moment. But make the daily choice to do the hard work, and bit by bit, allow love to be your loop flowing through all the negatives to positively relinquish the hurt and transfer possession to the Lord. He already made the promise to carry each of our burdens; we just must let go.

day 42.

MINI-MONY

Exodus 3:13-15

But Moses protested, "If I go to the people of Israel and tell them, 'The God of your ancestors has sent me to you,' they will ask me, 'What is his name?' Then what should I tell them?"

¹⁴God replied to Moses, "I am who I am. Say this to the people of Israel: I am has sent me to you."

¹⁵God also said to Moses, "Say this to the people of Israel: Yahweh, the God of your ancestors—the God of Abraham, the God of Isaac, and the God of Jacob—has sent me to you.
This is my eternal name,
my name to remember for all generations.

———————————————————————

Mini-testimony: Frame of reference goes beyond perspective; it is the criteria to determine value and judgment. It exceeds attitude or point of view by maintaining its position as the base. The last few weeks were challenging. There were moments my perspective caused change in my attitude and happiness. BUT a reminder found me in the Word of God, Exodus 3:14, "I AM that I AM." Even in moments of despair, my perspective may cause me to wonder "Why me?" "Why now?" Using the Word of God as a frame of reference reminded me that even in sadness, He is still all I need and more. Just as He assured Moses, He reassured me. And just like that, joy found its way to me again.

day 43.

THE ROYAL STANDARD

2 Timothy 2:15

Work hard so you can present yourself to God and receive his approval. Be a good worker, one who does not need to be ashamed and who correctly explains the word of truth.

We all have rules by which we govern ourselves, ideas upon which we base our decisions, and morals that serve as our compass navigating the world. We have standards—certain metric we hope to exist within. Anything below our typical standards can be looked at with criticism and sometimes disappointment; whereas, surpassing a standard or expectation allows us to be exposed to new heights and, consequently, an adjustment to our typical norms.

I have had this conversation more times than I can imagine. For example, I had a conversation with someone detailing how hard I am on myself. I set goals I hope to reach, mile markers I hope to hit, and things I hope to acquire. Although some goals are reasonable and some goals may seem radical, it is my metric. If I perform lower than normal, my dependability sways or stagnation occurs; I am already in self-reflective mode and wagging my finger in my face. Some people may call it overreacting. I call it accountability.

In another instance, I was counseling a person who was distraught about college courses. Through tears, she expressed the frustration of trying hard to excel and her efforts not producing the results she would like to see. I encouraged her by pointing out disappointment is a good sign. It showed she was not pleased with the results and would work tirelessly to make different outcomes next time. I would much rather see an uncomfortable person willing to adjust rather than a person contouring him or herself to stay in one place.

Lastly, I had a conversation with a lady who was determined to launch her own business. We chatted about opportunity, mindset, and the willingness to plow fields in the hopes of planting seeds and reaping a harvest. We discussed the boldness it takes to say, "Traditional is not for me" or "I don't want to work forty years at a job just because I am supposed to." We both agreed; traditional and common things do not always satisfy a person's standards. And that is okay.

Never apologize for your definition of excellence. Your expectations and standards give you something to strive towards and work for. They give you brackets to hold yourself accountable. Even if you slip or fail to hit them, do not lower them. You must climb until you make it.

And when you make it, build another ladder!

day 44.

IT'S YOUR THING

2 Thessalonians 1:11-12

So, we keep on praying for you, asking our God to enable you to live a life worthy of his call. May he give you the power to accomplish all the good things your faith prompts you to do.

[12] Then the name of our Lord Jesus will be honored because of the way you live, and you will be honored along with him. This is all made possible because of the grace of our God and Lord, Jesus Christ.

Everyone is different in his or her own way. We all have principles and morals by which we govern ourselves. We have "whys" we commonly use to justify our actions. We have stories to back our fears and reasoning to associate with assumptions and logic to step ahead of decisions. We all have our… "thing."

My "things" are relationship, servitude, and transparency. I try to abide by these three things daily for multiple reasons. Firstly, relationships matter to me, regardless of the type of relationship. I am a firm believer that each person deserves the honor, respect, and compassion of the next. Furthermore, I do not believe it to be deserved as much as I feel it to be owed. I know it is a nontraditional way of thinking. Typically, you hear people say, "Respect is earned." Although I believe it to be true in general, I think we should maintain responsibility in finding ways to love, whether we deem a person deserving or not, which brings me to my second pinnacle principle of servitude.

Servitude is not easy. It is a daily sacrifice to look beyond yourself, your own agenda, and your own desires with the sole purpose of seeing to the needs of people around you. It requires an attitude that replaces anger with a mindset to forgive and to try to stick to the mission of being an example of what God has called us all to be. It is not easy, nor is it everyone's strong suit. I, too, have my days when it is much easier said than done. At times, choosing this route seems to be an invitation to the world around you to test your LAST nerve. Even when that occurs, be honest enough with yourself to admit frustration, and focus on redirecting your emotions back to the mission, which is a perfect transition into transparency.

Honesty is something we all appreciate but rarely supply. Day to day, for whatever reason, we hold others to a standard of owing us the truth. Yet we hide how we really feel, what we really think, and what we are willing to do. Unfortunately, we give ourselves more credit than we are good for because often we are not fooling anyone. Rather than handling others and the space around us with transparency, we give act after act of Tony Award worthy performances. It creates an aura of fakeness and mistrust, doubt and despair. How will you ever create relationships with trust or be able to serve others in truth if you cannot even offer a true transparent version of yourself?

What are your pinnacle principles? Take today to evaluate yourself and the traits of yours that shine through more than others. After the observation, is it something of which you are proud? Do you need to work on yourself more? We are all far from perfect, but choosing who you will be daily is the first step to how people will receive you. Remember, days go by quickly. Your mission clock is winding down. How are you using your time? How are you impacting those around you? How are you doing "your thing?"

day 45.

WAIT…IT'S WORTH IT

Isaiah 55:8-9

"My thoughts are nothing like your thoughts," says the Lord.
"And my ways are far beyond anything you could imagine.

⁹For just as the heavens are higher than the earth,
so my ways are higher than your ways,
and my thoughts higher than your thoughts. …"

When God tells you to wait for His go-ahead, there is a reason. Regardless of how heavy you feel in the things you have held within, it is always wise to wait on Him to give approval. Prematurely entering conversations or decisions can create several issues with the largest of them being confusion. We have been given many examples in the Bible of God not being a God of confusion. He worked and continues to work with clear instructions and a plan of action. In doing so, it ensures confidence and peace.

Unfortunately, sometimes we get ahead of ourselves and are motivated by our emotions rather than our spiritual guidance. So, what happens when you "forget" to wait? You end up on the tail end, sorting through the "what if I said it like this instead of that?" "What if I did this rather than that?" "I hope they understood my point or intentions." But how to move forward? Simple.

You seek God and apologize for yielding to anxiousness rather than His will. You pray for Him to pardon you within the heart of the other person. You also pray He grants you peace within your own heart for your leap ahead. Many times, we hold our own guilt as punishment, never giving God a chance to restore.

I remember a sweet friend teaching me a valuable lesson I live by and of which I frequently remind myself: "Your feelings are yours to own, and they are justifiable." Your "whys" do not need to be accompanied by explanations to others, but they do require you to be honest with yourself about why they are what they are. You owe yourself to sort through yourself to discover the cause of your effects and emotions. If they require work on your end, then you owe yourself the construction period as well. Though the thing not to forget is God is the Licensed Contractor. He knows what things need to connect for healing to be true. He knows what wires may make you short circuit and which ones make you shine. Repair comes from the inside out, and rebuilding comes from the foundation.

Restoration along this journey of life is inevitable, but just like any other lesson learned, move forward in wisdom. Wait on the Lord for all things, and allow Him to make your way clear and peaceful.

day 46.

AND I WONDER, WHO'S LOVING YOU?

Colossians 3:12-17

Since God chose you to be the holy people He loves, you must clothe yourselves with tenderhearted mercy, kindness, humility, gentleness, and patience.

¹³Make allowance for each other's faults and forgive anyone who offends you. Remember, the Lord forgave you, so you must forgive others.

¹⁴Above all, clothe yourselves with love, which binds us all together in perfect harmony.

¹⁵And let the peace that comes from Christ rule in your hearts. For as members of one body you are called to live in peace. And always be thankful.

¹⁶Let the message about Christ, in all its richness, fill your lives. Teach and counsel each other with all the wisdom He gives. Sing psalms and hymns and spiritual songs to God with thankful hearts.

[17]And whatever you do or say, do it as a representative of the Lord Jesus, giving thanks through Him to God the Father.

There are small things in life the people who are closest to you do to show love. Every morning, for as long as I can remember, my father wakes up before my mother and me. After his morning devotion, he devotes his time to the three ladies in the house. Our dog, Ko-ko gets a special walk, my mother's coffee is in place on the dresser to cool before she wakes, and he turns the heater on in my bathroom to ensure ultimate comfort when I begin to get ready. These small details start the day with the silent but loudly heard affirmation of "I love you."

How do you say, "I love you," and how do you hear it? There are five love languages: words of affirmation, acts of service, receiving gifts, quality time, and physical touch. Each are different and are displayed differently depending on the person. Regardless of the how, the what is always the same. Be sure to appreciate the ones around you; show love, kindness, patience, and support.

day 47.

IN DARKNESS COMES THE LIGHT

John 8:12

Jesus spoke to the people once more and said, "I am the light of the world. If you follow me, you won't have to walk in darkness, because you will have the light that leads to life."

It is funny how God works. Follow me on a journey of my day so far.

One morning, I was awakened by God before the sun even lifted. I usually do not like these early morning calls because He wants to talk. In the past, the conversations have been interesting. He usually enlightens me as I lie in the darkness of my room. Some conversations have birthed ideas while others have granted revelations. Some talks bring smiles while others bring tears. I treasure them all.

It is pitch-black in my room, and He simply says, "Listen and watch me." I lay, I waited, I prayed, I tried to sleep and still could not. So, I lay there in the presence of Him.

I will admit, around six o'clock, my wait became frustrating, and I became restless. I prayed for peace to find me. Then, I slipped into slumber. Maybe ten minutes later, a text arrived. It read, "Good morning, Bianca! Feet on the floor. Eyes on God. You are on duty. Whole armor ready!" I giggled in amazement because the ONLY time this person texts me is when I hit a wall. She is always timely in delivering His assignment to me.

After reading it, I put my feet on the ground and began to prepare for church. The phone rang, and a friend asked if I could pick her up for church. We talked as I approached her house, and I learned she, too, had a night that did not include much sleep. She got in the car, and we continued to talk about how God enters our quiet spaces and darkest moments to heal our hearts and calm our deepest woes.

We talked so much until I completely missed Sunday school, but God's glory was still visible. One of my students gave the review and spoke of how God used the stars to encourage Abraham concerning what the future held in store. In response, I shouted on the inside because God makes no mistakes. I missed teaching the lesson, but He used a student to speak to me. Because, you see, if God used stars to illustrate His promise, it means He met

Abraham at night. HE talked to him at night!

But wait! That same weekend, my father celebrated his fifty-fifth birthday out of town. I heard him voice a concern of the quality of the message because he could not study as much as he typically would. Boy, was he wrong! As he stood to inform the congregation of the scriptures, the title came across the screen, and I laughed again, "In Darkness, there Comes the Light." The whole sermon was about trusting your darkness is not the end y'all; it is the wait before the shine. Even in the dark, trusting God means knowing He is still there—meaning, if you lay awake in the night and He says listen and watch, it does not have to be an immediate answer to be God. Rather than feeling lost, alone, or blinded, know you can still see His glory.

I hear it loudly and clearly: Feet on the floor. Eyes on God. You are on duty. Whole armor ready!

day 48.

DEFINERS

Hebrews 13:6-7

*So, we can say with confidence,
"The Lord is my helper,
so, I will have no fear.
What can mere people do to me?"*

[7]Remember your leaders who taught you the word of God. Think of all the good that has come from their lives and follow the example of their faith.

I recently heard a speaker give these Three Tips for Leadership and Joy:

1. Operate with Integrity. Even when it is a challenge,

choose to be the best version of yourself. You will end the day with no remorse or regret.

2. Operate with Intelligence. Be bold in what you know. Make wise decisions. Do not base your choices on the comfort of others if it means clipping your wings or sacrificing a chance to learn more, grow your horizons, or advance your joy.

3. Operate to Inspire. At the end of each day, you should be able to identify something that inspired you. It means you have observed the world around you and decided to find joy in even the bleakest of days. When you have found "that thing," try to inspire someone else as well.

Try to commit to this thought process, and see if it makes a difference. You've got this!

day 49.

OCEANS

Psalm 29:1-3

*Honor the Lord, you heavenly beings;
honor the Lord for His glory and strength.*

*²Honor the Lord for the glory of His name.
Worship the Lord in the splendor of His holiness.*

*³The voice of the Lord echoes above the sea.
The God of glory thunders.
The Lord thunders over the mighty sea.*

Have you ever gone to the beach, walked along the shore, and enjoyed the waves as they came closer to tickle your toes for a few seconds before being drawn back in? Have you ever found yourself adjusting to the temperature to go a little deeper until the waves are at your ankles, then calves, then waist? It is about at this level when you are more likely to be caught off-guard by a stronger wave. It rushes in larger than you saw coming, and it slightly tugs you forward.

Life is an ocean of things, filled with different types of experiences, lessons, and people. There are shallow times, deeper times, beauty, and danger. Sometimes life comes at you quickly. One moment you are enjoying its pleasantries while at other times you must re-establish your footing. Either way, just as the ocean, life goes on.

Never allow the depths of life or the height of the waves cause you to forget the certainty of tides. Keep your balance, and enjoy every bit of the experience.

TURNING WOUNDS INTO WISDOM

James 1:2-5

Dear brothers and sisters, when troubles of any kind come your way, consider it an opportunity for great joy.

³For you know that when your faith is tested, your endurance has a chance to grow.

⁴So let it grow, for when your endurance is fully developed, you will be perfect and complete, needing nothing.

⁵If you need wisdom, ask our generous God, and He will give it to you. He will not rebuke you for asking.

What has hurt you lately? And what did you do with that pain?

Oprah suggests we must all "Turn [our] wounds into wisdom."

Pain is hard to process. It can make us react physically, mentally, and emotionally. And nothing is wrong with that; in fact, it is normal. What you do after processing makes all the difference in the person you become after the incident.

We must learn not to allow our pain to beat us down and count us out. We must choose to stand tall and apply its lesson as wisdom.

Wisdom is a unique trait. Wisdom is knowing the difference. Wisdom is the ability to discern and judge which aspects of experiences are true, right, lasting, and applicable to your life. It is the ability to apply the knowledge to the greater scheme of life. It is also deeper. It is knowing the meaning or reason. It is about knowing why something is and what it means to your life.

Life is a journey, so bumps and bruises are inevitable. Always find a way to turn your wounds into wisdom and enjoy the trail anyhow!

day 51.

CHANGING COMPLAINTS TO CLAIMS

Philippians 2:14-18

Do everything without complaining and arguing,

[15]so that no one can criticize you. Live clean, innocent lives as children of God, shining like bright lights in a world full of crooked and perverse people.

[16]Hold firmly to the word of life; then, on the day of Christ's return, I will be proud that I did not run the race in vain and that my work was not useless.

[17]But I will rejoice even if I lose my life, pouring it out like a liquid offering to God, just like your faithful service is an offering to God. And I want all of you to share that joy.

[18]Yes, you should rejoice, and I will share your joy.

I recently read something that read "To spend your life complaining about the things you don't like is equivalent to going to a restaurant and telling the waiter all the things you don't want to eat."

Powerful, right? Life is not assumed to be perfect. Of course, there will be things that frustrate you, things with which you don't agree, experiences you would've rather not witnessed, or even people you could have done without, but how do you respond to those things. Do you complain and obsessively critique? Do you learn and readjust?

Life is a series of decisions we must make coupled with chance and happenings. Beyond that, it is our reactions. Our responses can make or break who we become. Remember, at the end of the day, we should be very selective regarding that to which we give our energy. Life is too short to waste its most precious moments.

Take what you can from each moment, learn from it all, and respond with CLAIMING your moments rather than COMPLAINING!

day 52.

LET YOUR SPARK IGNITE

Romans 12:11-18

Never be lazy but work hard and serve the Lord enthusiastically.

[12]Rejoice in our confident hope. Be patient in trouble and keep on praying.

[13]When God's people are in need, be ready to help them. Always be eager to practice hospitality.

[14]Bless those who persecute you. Don't curse them; pray that God will bless them.

[15]Be happy with those who are happy, and weep with those who weep.

[16]Live in harmony with each other. Don't be too proud to enjoy the company of ordinary people. And don't think you know it all!

[17]*Never pay back evil with more evil. Do things in such a way that everyone can see you are honorable.*

[18]*Do all that you can to live in peace with everyone.*

Today's wisdom is simply said but takes work… LET YOUR SPARK IGNITE. It can easily be forgotten when we are tired, feel as if life has more "meh" moments than mesmerizing ones, or when we feel a little dull.

It takes only a small spark to light a fire. There is a real challenge to start a fire without a spark so much so until you cannot start a fire without a spark. The spark requires a certain level of patience and calm. Both are good practices when attempting to start your fire.

In colonial America, flint and steel were used to light fires. Both are tools that are tough and the definition of grit. Google defines grit as "courage and resolve; strength of character" when used as a noun and as "a clench (the teeth), especially in order to keep one's resolve when faced with an unpleasant or painful duty" when defined as a verb.

Likewise, we must be tough despite what happens around us and regardless of how discouraging it can be. We must endure and keep grinding until the spark ignites and catches on to our other resources to make a fire. Once it happens, you shine, shine, shine, and maintain your fire. It will serve as a signal to others of your presence. It is proof of your hard work and tireless efforts and will provide you with warmth on cold days and will shine light in your darkest moments.

Let your spark ignite; it will grow into vivid brilliance!

day 53.

MOUNTAIN HIGH, VALLEY LOW

Psalm 23

*The Lord is my shepherd;
I have all that I need.*

*[2]He lets me rest in green meadows;
He leads me beside peaceful streams.*

*[3]He renews my strength.
He guides me along right paths,
bringing honor to His name.*

*[4]Even when I walk
through the darkest valley,
I will not be afraid,
for You are close beside me.
Your rod and Your staff
protect and comfort me.*

bianca chandler

*⁵You prepare a feast for me
in the presence of my enemies.
You honor me by anointing my head with oil.
My cup overflows with blessings.*

*⁶Surely Your goodness and unfailing love will pursue me
all the days of my life,
and I will live in the house of the Lord
forever.*

Have you ever heard of a mountain top experience versus a valley experience? Usually when these references are made, it is insinuated the mountain top hints at accomplishment, success, and admiration whereas a valley is viewed as a low point of despair, sadness, and failure. Is such an assumption truly accurate?

Most valleys are areas with their own levels of beauty. They keep the mountain grounded, are home to lush greenery and plant life, host calm streams, and are technically a created wonder. In life, we categorize our lower moments as an issue rather than a space to grow. We miss the beauty around us by being more concerned with wishing we were atop a mountain. We hide beneath the shadows of trees in shame when we could learn a lesson of blooming right where we are. We miss the moments of peace and tranquility that can be used to restore because we are too busy plotting our next climb.

Then there is the mountain. The part of the story that sounds just as triumphant as it is large. Yes, everyone wants mountain top experiences, but are you truly ready for the work? Are you willing to toil even when you are tired? Are you willing to go even when a forceful wind passes by? Reach when it hurts? Trust past the fog? Ignore the passing of the birds and not tremble in fear when you are far from what you know? Endure when your hands are gritty? Breathe when the pressure gets tough? Can you stand once you are there?

The mountain is often glorified, but it requires hard work. The valley is looked down upon but has so much opportunity to growth and preparation. Whether you are climbing a mountain or walking the valley, you are right where you were meant to be. Enjoy it all!

day 54.

SUCCESS IS…

Matthew 6:19-21

Don't store up treasures here on earth, where moths eat them and rust destroys them, and where thieves break in and steal.

[20]Store your treasures in heaven, where moths and rust cannot destroy, and thieves do not break in and steal.

[21]Wherever your treasure is, there the desires of your heart will also be.

Arthur F. Lenehan is the author of The Best of Bits & Pieces, which is a collection of the most loved and requested anecdotes, quotes, touches of humor, bits of wisdom, and success stories from his well-known magazine. He is quoted in it, saying,

"Success in life should be determined by contributions not accumulations."

Some people get it. They understand everything in life is bigger than them. They understand the importance of giving, supporting, and contributing to the world around them. Other people—not so much. They become so distracted by receiving, focusing on themselves, and collecting things from people until they never advance. Although it may seem selfish at first glance, it is not always their fault. Sometimes life throws a wrench our way, and it affects our perspective, how we love, or even how we share ourselves. We become so guarded and fearful that we only extend ourselves to grab but fail to give.

Living a shared life is a very scary but beautiful thing. It requires a certain level of vulnerability that says, "Here I am… come and get me!" Sometimes it fares out well, and sometimes it does not. As I have said before, life is a series of things that happen; the pivotal moment is how we respond. Rather than allowing your perspective to become negative, find a way to give of yourself in spite of your gloom.

Let us use the rest of this week to evaluate our ratio of contribution to accumulation.

Take time to identify which person you are.

Do you measure your success by the material things you conclude your day with or the parts of you that supply substance to others?

How can you move towards the latter?

day 55.

WHO ARE YOU REALLY?

1 Samuel 16:7

But the Lord said to Samuel, "Do not look on his appearance or on the height of his stature, because I have rejected him. For the Lord sees not as a man sees; man looks on the outward appearance, but the Lord looks on the heart."

I once took an online personality assessment called, 16 Personalities. A few years after taking the personality assessment, I took it again, and to my amazement, the results were the same.

The super cool thing about this assessment is how accurate it is.

At the end of the test, you will fall into one of the four largest categories. You will be pegged as either an Analyst, Diplomat, Sentinel, or an Explorer; each category has four sub-categories that accompany your personality type.

Here is where it gets interesting! This computer program has never met you personally, yet somehow it transforms your answers into shockingly accurate data, covering your strengths and weaknesses, romantic relationships, friendships, parenthood, career paths, workplace habits, and a polite conclusion that leaves your jaw dropped.

It made me think of something. Many of us have an idea of who we are…. we may even have a good handle on knowing whose we are. We know what interests us, what triggers us, what motivates us—even our flaws. Every so often, in knowing those things, we choose to hide them or fail to acknowledge them at all. At the end of the day, the truth is it contributes to who you are. Knowing yourself and acknowledging all of you can be the determining factor of your success. You must be honest and transparent with yourself before you can expect anyone else to buy into you or your dreams.

day 56.

YOU.

Romans 8:1-2

So now there is no condemnation for those who belong to Christ Jesus.

²And because you belong to Him, the power of the life-giving Spirit has freed you from the power of sin that leads to death.

One of my good friends gave me an entire box of quotes. I do not think she really knows just how precious it is to me, but for a very long time, I have valued words. I value their ability to transform situations just by being uttered, the power they must inspire, and even how a lack thereof still speaks volumes. Well, each day I pick one to be my strength for the day. One morning, the quote came from Henri Nouwan, and it reads, "In solitude we discover that our life is not a possession to be defended, but a gift to be shared."

Sometimes we all are guilty of owning our truths for the wrong reasons. We acknowledge the parts in which we take pride but boldly defend them to guard the truths we do not want others to see. Often it is not even about our visibility to others as much as it is us hiding ourselves from ourselves.

Nikolai Ostrovsky is quoted with "Man's dearest possession is life. It is given to him but once, and he must live it so as to feel no torturing regrets for wasted years, never know the burning shame of a mean and petty past; so live that, dying, he might say: all my life, all my strength were given to the finest cause in all the world—the fight for the Liberation of Mankind." Life is our greatest possession. A thing none of us asked for but all so blessed to have.

How much of yourself are you defending daily rather than giving? Be sure not to pick and choose which parts of you matter enough to be shared. All of it matters—the good, the bad, and the ugly. The best part about admitting fault is the opportunity of reconcilement. The best part about recognizing flaw is the ability to accept. The best part about both is the example you can be to inspire someone else to do the same.

Choose today to reconcile, accept, and share all the amazing things about you that makes life a gift.

day 57.

TRY. STRIVE. THRIVE.

Luke 11:5-13

Then, teaching them more about prayer, he used this story: "Suppose you went to a friend's house at midnight, wanting to borrow three loaves of bread. You say to him,

[6]'A friend of mine has just arrived for a visit, and I have nothing for him to eat.'

[7]And suppose he calls out from his bedroom, 'Don't bother me. The door is locked for the night, and my family and I are all in bed. I can't help you.'

[8]But I tell you this—though he won't do it for friendship's sake, if you keep knocking long enough, he will get up and give you whatever you need because of your shameless persistence.

[9]"And so I tell you, keep on asking, and you will receive what you ask for. Keep on seeking, and you will find. Keep on knocking, and the door will be opened to you.

¹⁰For everyone who asks, receives. Everyone who seeks, finds. And to everyone who knocks, the door will be opened.

¹¹"You fathers—if your children ask for a fish, do you give them a snake instead?

¹²Or if they ask for an egg, do you give them a scorpion? Of course not!

¹³So if you sinful people know how to give good gifts to your children, how much more will your heavenly Father give the Holy Spirit to those who ask him."

We all try, strive, and thrive daily to be a better person than we were yesterday. Some days, the task can be easier than others.

I have six tips for you to try as checkpoints throughout the day: identification, qualification, cultivation, solicitation, acknowledgment, and stewardship.

Start each day with identification of yourself. Do an inventory of your gifts and talents to challenge the day head-on. Your gifts are tools intended to help you to take pride in who you are while serving others.

Next, remember you are qualified. Because your gifts are yours to claim, it is your right to utilize them throughout the day to connect to the world around you and make positive change.

Then there is cultivation. Committing to the idea of utilizing what is already within you gives you a chance to practice and grow even more. You can triumph because of your willingness to try!

Solicitation sometimes carries a negative connotation, but it does not mean to beg—only to ask. Be inquisitive. Seek opportunities to learn. Never look over a lesson, especially not by overlooking a person.

Next up, acknowledgment. Be big enough to admit fault, congratulate others, and be humble. In doing so, you become a good steward.

Do you remember what we talked about in the stage of stewardship? Life is a gift. Be sure to treat it (as well as other people's lives) as such. Take time to do self-assessments and correct areas when necessary.
It is all a part of the journey!

day 58.

JUST BLOOM

Luke 6:30-36

Give to anyone who asks; and when things are taken away from you, don't try to get them back.

³¹Do to others as you would like them to do to you.

³²"If you love only those who love you, why should you get credit for that? Even sinners love those who love them!

³³And if you do good only to those who do good to you, why should you get credit? Even sinners do that much!

³⁴And if you lend money only to those who can repay you, why should you get credit? Even sinners will lend to other sinners for a full return.

³⁵Love your enemies! Do good to them. Lend to them without expecting to be repaid. Then your reward from heaven will be very great, and you will truly be acting as children of the Most High, for he is kind to those who are unthankful and wicked.

[36]You must be compassionate, just as your Father is compassionate. ..."

One of my television obsessions is called A Million Little Things.

It is a beautifully written show that follows the journey of friendships, marriages, joys, and even unexpected complexities. One of the characters said something that stood out to me in reference to relationships. She said something along the lines of "Sometimes you're the gardener when it should be your turn to be the flower." Some people naturally care for other people while others are naturally cared for.

It can be instinctual, a created norm, or maybe just contingent upon the day and the time. It does not make one person better than the next nor stronger than the next.

It simply means two different roles. Both offer their own beauty.

A gardener's beauty lies in the patience of nurturing. Their ability to know just how to provide what a plant needs. They are likely very familiar with the flower, things to which it can become vulnerable, that by which it needs to be surrounded, and even knowing when to serve up tough love. It is not always the most visible part but very necessary.

A flower's beauty can be found in its ability to be groomed—their humbleness to allow a person to know so much about them, allowing them to interact with their most vulnerable pieces and having enough trust to be cradled by a gardener's care—it is in this process their visibility becomes unmissable.

Although wonderful, both should take caution. Gardeners can sometimes become so dedicated to the crop they forget to allow anyone to take care of them. With the same commitment it takes to learn and serve, remember you deserve to receive. Flowers remember to offer a beauty to the world that humbleness allows to grow. Never be apologetic for being favored. It is a gift.

I challenge you to figure out which role you play in your interactions with people. Remember whether you are the planter or the planted, and just bloom.

day 59.

WHY CAN'T YOU WALK?

Titus 2:7-8

And you yourself must be an example to them by doing good works of every kind. Let everything you do reflect the integrity and seriousness of your teaching.

[8]Teach the truth so that your teaching can't be criticized. Then those who oppose us will be ashamed and have nothing bad to say about us.

A lot of my work involves youth. I hope to help them understand life can be challenging, overwhelming at times, and downright frustrating; it is important to still give life your all and persevere. Sometimes these frustrations will make it easier to make excuses rather than an attempt to change. Sometimes people will draw conclusions of your capabilities based on where you come from or who they think you are likely to become without getting to know you. Occasionally, they will shield the truth because it is more convenient to their agenda or level of comfort for you to be left in the dark. As a result, it is vital to understand the importance of hard work and maximizing opportunities. I used this analogy to aid in illustration.

Hypothetically, let us say there is a baby—born healthy, developing as he or she should, alert, and full of life. He or she is approaching the stage of development when he or she is moving around more and ready to master walking. Upon the first few attempts, he or she stumbles and falls. The baby's cries are overheard by the mom who just cannot stand to see her baby fall. She promises Baby she will carry him or her until he or she is ready.

On the first day of preschool she carries Baby in, places him or her in a chair, and turns to the teacher to inform her that Baby does not walk. Taken aback, the teacher pauses but does not want to challenge the new information and assures mom she will make sure all is well.

A few years later, Baby begins fifth grade five. Mom wheels Baby into class to a desk where the teacher is already informed of the accommodations and needs of Baby. She introduces Baby to the other members of the class and sets the tone for expected behavior and acceptance of Baby's differences. Later down the road, Baby wheels across the stage for graduation to the applause of others.

Then comes college. Baby is in a group of new friends who are interested in his or her story. They ask, "Baby, we understand you are in a wheelchair, but we're just curious—why can't you walk?" Baby pauses to think about it and has no answer beyond "Well, it has always been this way."

You see, we as society have created a lot of children like "Baby" who grow to be adults who make more "Babies." We groom them according to what is comfortable for us. We try to protect them from the things around them all while blocking needed lessons and opportunities. What is worse is we pass them on to the next people with false realities. We cut out the chance to grow in new areas because they enter with a limited version of themselves surrounded by accommodations. The tainted truth eventually precedes the person. All while it is happening, "Baby" accepts it all as the only life he or she knows. Consequently, the potential to move forward is not completely removed, but it is not the natural progression. Just as muscles will begin to deteriorate so will ambition. They become reliant on other resources or people to carry them through. Until one day, something comes along that challenges them to think differently and choose if it is the day, they will put in the rehab work to regain control or submit to what narrative has been written for them and stay seated.

Who is controlling your life? Are you on your feet or in a seat? Think about it.

day 60.

IN THE SWING OF THINGS

Psalm 118:24

*This is the day the Lord has made.
We will rejoice and be glad in it.*

How do you start your day? I pray, stretch, and begin to ready myself for the day. It is always interesting to me how our routines are so engrained in us. We become creatures of habit before we even know it. While this can seemingly be harmless, it can also create stagnation.

Google says routines are a sequence of actions regularly followed, a fixed program. It is also performed as part of a regular procedure rather than for a special reason. My question to you today is the same I often ask myself: "Can all my days remain like this?"

Passion should greet your feet as they hit the floor in the morning. Your purpose should be the push behind you as you navigate the day. Look for the unexpected and celebrate it as it arrives. Rejoice in routine shifts as it is a good suggestion of a life being lived rather than a life programmed. Find ways to inject your character and charisma into the people around you while being sure to soak in their awesomeness as well.

Life is not meant to be a pattern downloaded and run daily; it is meant to be experienced through impact and exchange.

Make living your daily routine!

day 61.

MISSION AND MOTIVE

Galatians 6:9-10

So, let's not get tired of doing what is good. At just the right time we will reap a harvest of blessing if we don't give up.

¹⁰Therefore, whenever we have the opportunity, we should do good to everyone—especially to those in the family of faith.

Today, I want to start with two questions. What is your mission, and what is your motive? I want to issue you a challenge. When you wake in the morning, take the time to establish or think about your mission, and allow it to become your motive.

Occasionally, we are discouraged by realizing our mistakes, and it distracts us from our mission. But be encouraged and remember mistakes are inevitable. No one is perfect. Do not allow a flounder to misguide your mission or discredit your motives.

Secondly, we all must live for impact. What you do daily should be felt daily by others. I recently challenged myself to reflect and observe what parts of me were people experiencing most often. I went further to wonder "If I never met this person again, what would his or her last encounter with me look like?" Wow.

That brings us to legacy. That last encounter, or the ones prior to it, determine your legacy to that specific person. What are you working towards? What will be able to speak for you even when you are no longer present to advocate for yourself or your efforts?

You have the power to not only control your own decisions in action and response, but you have the power to contribute to how other people are inspired along their journeys. Be open to learning from mistakes, be kind even when you are not in the mood, be a life that ends in legacy. Let that be your mission; let that be your motive.

day 62.

LIFE IS ART

Habakkuk 2:1

*I will climb up to my watchtower,
and stand at my guard post.
There I will wait to see what the Lord says
and how he will answer my complaint.*

Life is art. It is all about awareness, relationship, and transparency. Often, we become so involved in things until we lose our pace, form habits, or become so comfortable to the point we are not as observant as we once were. We develop a tunnel vision that only sees straight, and we call it focus. But that is not always true. Focus still requires a certain level of awareness, which is defined as knowledge or perception of a situation or fact.

Be alert and conscious of what things happen around you. Never miss out on an opportunity because you were not positioned to receive. You cannot discover higher heights with a perspective that only sees at ground level. Likewise, you cannot grow or learn from others when you interact with blinded eyes and deafened ears. Listen and see! And that brings me to relationship.

A lot of us miss out on opportunities if it means having to interact with others or trust others. Do not allow experiences you have had in the past to forge how you move forward in building relationships with others. The point of pain is to protect through feelings and experience. In the experience, we are not supposed to treat all future risks as dead-end signs but as caution signs. You slow down, observe (that is awareness again), and climb over the obstacle. Be real with where you are, with who you encounter, and your own self!

That is why transparency is so important! Be brave enough to be clear enough. Speak up and say what you have observed. Speak up and say what pain you have experienced and are fearful of being repeated. Be honest about your experiences and how they have contributed to who you are. Claim your life and proclaim it as your truth.

Life is not about perfection. It is about how you display all the wonderful things that make you who you are. It is your textures, vibrancy, lines, abstractness, uniqueness—it is you.

day 63.

BREAK FREE

Matthew 18:15-18

If another believer sins against you, go privately and point out the offense. If the other person listens and confesses it, you have won that person back.

16But if you are unsuccessful, take one or two others with you and go back again, so that everything you say may be confirmed by two or three witnesses.

17If the person still refuses to listen, take your case to the church. Then if he or she won't accept the church's decision, treat that person as a pagan or a corrupt tax collector.

18"I tell you the truth, whatever you forbid on earth will be forbidden in heaven, and whatever you permit on earth will be permitted in heaven. ..."

Today let us talk about the things that bind us. Often, we drag around this weight, and it limits our ability to soar to our highest heights. We become so familiar with this weight we build a level of strength and tolerance. It allows us to carry it well enough to not even stumble or limp. The problem is tolerance is not the same as triumph.

So what is the weight? The weight can be multiple things. It can be fear, shame, guilt, unresolved hurt, or insecurities—all of which are rooted in the dark, abysmal ignorance of who you really are. Knowing yourself, your desires, your passions, your strengths, and even your weaknesses can become the universal key to every lock securing the chains around you as well as the key to unlock every door before you.

Do not allow things that have happened to you define you. They are simply experiences, which contributed to who you are but are not what solidifies your existence. We learn to live with guilt and shame rather than owning what is real and denying what is not. We give our insecurities a voice by giving in to the lies of unworthiness or insufficiency. We allow fear to captain a ship that faith should command. We allow our hurt to become a fatal affliction rather than a healed wound. We tolerate rather than triumph.

Focus on finding the keys to freeing yourself. Higher skies await you.

day 64.

TIGHTROPE

1 Corinthians 15:58

So, my dear brothers and sisters, be strong and immovable. Always work enthusiastically for the Lord, for you know that nothing you do for the Lord is ever useless.

Here is a story for you. I have been struggling in different ways—struggling to decide how to express myself without seeming like a complainer and struggling to promote content as a motivator while also trying to find ways to keep myself motivated. Stress has manifested itself in loss of sleep, forgetfulness, and body aches. So I decided to take charge and find a way to balance it all.

A few years ago, Janelle Monae wrote a song entitled, "Tightrope." She talks about the criticism of others, their expectations, their observance, and paints this analogy that whether you are high or low, you still have to find your balance and be able to perform. I thought about it. A lot of us are good at putting aside how we feel, jumping into our costumed roles, climbing to heights that people "ohhhh" and "awwww" at, lining up, shaking off our own woes, and performing. Day after day we show up for the show. We become experts at finding a way to balance these things. Without the balance, there is the very evident danger of falling hard.

There is nothing wrong with admitting things have slipped from your control, but you cannot stop at admitting. You have to be willing to do the work to climb, re-center yourself, reset, and recommit. The funny thing is, we were never meant to be in control—only to follow God's will His way.

As far as heights go, I am far from where I want to be but just where I am supposed to be. I am learning to find joy in that place and perform my very best. I am learning not to add too much pressure. I am my own worst critic, and you can be, too.

Find a way to let go and let God.

day 65.

WAR CRY

Psalm 144:1-2

Praise the Lord, who is my rock.
He trains my hands for war
and gives my fingers skill for battle.

²He is my loving ally and my fortress,
my tower of safety, my rescuer.
He is my shield, and I take refuge in him.
He makes the nations submit to me.

Thanks to my pops I am a huge fan of movies like Gladiator, Troy, and 300. To this day, if any of the three come on, I find a seat on the sofa and hunker down. They are classic movies, and they capture the essence of ancient battle. Each movie tells a different tale, but all of them include a massive war scene. The main characters plot and plan schemes to overcome the enemy—whether it be in a rush, front facing, or a decoyed ambush. But one thing amazes me each time; regardless of the attack, it is preceded by a war cry.

So here you have it. An entire army of men with armor guarding their bodies and rage lining their chests. They fall into formation with the bravest on the frontlines—sustaining the right, left, and center wing; the strongest are tucked closely behind with light infantry and skilled archery, the ones with endurance to charge after the first fleet only steps beyond, and the reserves who await the beckoning call.

In formation, before the battle begins, the armies line up to measure up. They compare and spew, taunt and tantalize, and then it happens—the war cry. A leader ignites the call that will then echo in masses to those who stand before them once, then again, then once more before the charge.

It is a sound of warning the first time, the second resonates as an affirmed announcement of surety, and the last as the battle begins.

Life brings us battles. Some may seem bigger than others. Some may seem to last longer than others. Some come with forewarning while others seem to be a sneak attack. Yet remember this: your battles are already won. Fall into formation and scream your war cry with all your might. Yell once to warn the world you know no fear, yell twice to remind them of who you are and what kingdom you serve, and yell the last time as you challenge it head-on because its already done!

day 66.

LIVE FOR LEGACY

Psalm 112:1-3

Praise the Lord!
How joyful are those who fear the Lord
and delight in obeying his commands.

²Their children will be successful everywhere;
an entire generation of godly people will be blessed.

³They themselves will be wealthy,
and their good deeds will last forever.

If today was your last day, what is the story that your life would tell?

What moments would become the magic that make your life legendary?

Which of your contributions would compel others to ensure you were remembered?

Which of your bold acts would keep a fire burning for the coldest parts of the world to find hope?

What does it take to build a legacy that endures?

It takes two very frequently mentioned things and one thing that requires a humble courage none dares to obtain.

Stick with me.

The first is BOLDNESS.
Boldness is defined as a willingness to take risks and act innovatively—to do so with confidence or courage.

Be bold even when you are not sure where to begin or how things will end. Walk lines between hatred and hope. Whisper wisdom to the weary, and defended those close to defeat. Encourage coexistence in the midst of chaos. Understand that impact does not require impulse and that worthwhile change requires waiting.

Do you want to build an enduring legacy? Live in boldness.

The second is DETERMINATION.
Determination is defined as firmness of purpose—resoluteness.

It is also defined as the process of establishing something exactly by calculation or research.

Be determined and intentional. Legacy must be paired with a plan, a plan with a process, and a process focused on purpose. Your life must be more about how people experience what you contribute outwardly rather than what you inwardly experience. Do not allow the pressures of the world cause you to sulk or sway. Be firm and foundational for the weak who will find strength in your presence.

You must maintain a level of resolve that acts rationally even when provoked to rage. Take the time to learn strategies that make you successful. If you do not understand a concept, seek knowledge, welcome critique, and be adaptable to change. Know your strengths, for they will one day double as your weakness. When you meet that day, remember which of the traits within you made it a strength. Once you find that place, get up, dust yourself off, and continue. Life does not keep score of the amounts of times you may fall, but your success is scored by how many times you rise.

Do you want to build an enduring legacy? Labor with determination.

The third piece is the most important yet the hardest to commit to.

Before I jump into it, let us say what legacy is not. It is not pride, deceit, greed, selfishness, envy, arrogance, nor complacency. It cannot shrink itself down but dares not to amplify itself either. It will not back down and never misses an opportunity to stand up. It should not compare or compromise. It is willpower—simply the power to be willing.

The third is a willingness to be broken.
Willingness is defined as ready, eager, or prepared to do something.

You want to build a legacy, you say? You want to be known, remembered, and deemed important? The most valuable thing to remember is legacy is achieved when you completely remove you from the situation. When it is only your work that gives voice, only your impact that still screams, only your reach that still sings, only your generosity that still sews, only your pebble that ripples across the vastness of life.

Do you want to build a legacy? Remove you, just build.

day 67.

BRICK HOUSE

Jeremiah 18:1-6

The Lord gave another message to Jeremiah. He said,

²"Go down to the potter's shop, and I will speak to you there."

³So I did as He told me and found the potter working at his wheel.

⁴But the jar he was making did not turn out as he had hoped, so he crushed it into a lump of clay again and started over.

⁵Then the Lord gave me this message:

⁶"O Israel, can I not do to you as this potter has done to his clay? As the clay is in the potter's hand, so are you in My hand."

_____

I have a slight fascination with bricks. They have qualities that amaze me from the beginning of production to the way they age. I find a certain mystique in their ability to be similar yet different. Brittle yet solid. Sharp yet smooth. Compact yet mighty.

In creation, bricks go through a few phases. The dirt is first collected, then goes through a grinding process. Water is then added to change its consistency. The paste is then molded with tools, shaped into its familiar molds, and then left to bake in the sun to dry.

We are a lot like bricks. Life is a process. It requires us to go through phases. We are all remnants of things that have come before us—our past family members, traditions, and culture all gathered up into contributing to who we are today. Then life happens, and we experience our own ups and downs; some feel like shifting, some feel like glorious creation, and some feel like grinding. Regardless of how you feel or how you are changed, life still progresses, which means you have not reached your final form.

Just like bricks, things are added to us to change our consistency. While taking new shapes, we are also able to be refreshed and graced with second chances to represent ourselves to others in a more solidified way. Again, we do not stop at the grinding and have not yet reached the molding, but it is all in the process. When we allow God to mold us into better things, we become part of a community that reminds us we all come from dirt but have the chance to become so much more. As you know, bricks are not meant to stand alone. They are meant to be together to provide strength and refuge, shelter and character, stability and longevity. We are stronger together.

In the end, the gruesome process is rewarded with moments in the sun. We shine, we glow, and we come out stronger than ever.

day 68.

PROTECT YOUR SPACE

1 Corinthians 10:23-24

You say, "I am allowed to do anything"—but not everything is good for you. You say, "I am allowed to do anything"—but not everything is beneficial.

[24]Don't be concerned for your own good but for the good of others.

I have always had a special fondness for NASA. Well, if I am to be completely honest, it was a bit of a fascination. NASA's enduring purpose is scientific discovery and exploration for the benefit of the United States and humanity. I still vividly remember going to the NASA space museum and being completely enthralled in the history, the commitment, the curiosity, and the caliber of person one must be to even be considered for such an honor.

All these things matter because you do not just send any regular person into space. You send a person who knows their stuff. You send a person who is willing to go through the turbulence. Someone who can remain calm as they feel the impact of breaking what others consider to be bounding limits. You send a person who holds the courage to step out and experience rather than just observe from the ground. Furthermore, you send a person who is willing to stick to the mission regardless of the length of time.

By this point, you might be saying, "Bianca, what you're saying makes no sense." But stick with me! We must be our own NASA. It is imperative we monitor whom we allow into our own space. Too many of us have allowed people to take a front seat and buckle in, and they do not belong on our life's mission. They have invaded our potential with negativity and criticism and do not have the required skills to help us elevate from where we are.
Rather than treating our experiences as a conditioning phase, they complain of time wasted. They would rather watch and report than to assist and uplift. And as soon as things start to signal a beginning, rather than acknowledging the smoke as preparation for launch, they shudder in fear of destruction. At the first signs of effort being required, rather than maintaining focus, they flake.

Regardless of the contribution, every successful space mission has been made up of a team whose members all have the same goal in mind—discovery for the benefit of others.

Protect your space and focus on the mission.

There is a world depending on your life's mission to be a success.

day 69.

YOUR JUNK IS SHOWING

Ecclesiastes 3:1-6

For everything there is a season,
a time for every activity under heaven.

²A time to be born and a time to die.
A time to plant and a time to harvest.

³A time to kill and a time to heal.
A time to tear down and a time to build up.

⁴A time to cry and a time to laugh.
A time to grieve and a time to dance.

⁵A time to scatter stones and a time to gather stones.
A time to embrace and a time to turn away.

⁶A time to search and a time to quit searching.

bianca chandler

A time to keep and a time to throw away.

Today, let us get vulnerable. Let us have a moment of truth. Every house has the drawer. You know the drawer—the one where you throw everything that fits in it and just jam it closed. It is the place you go to for random paper clips, rubber bands, a AAA battery, a bag clip, the business card from the tax guy you met at Shoney's when Shoney's was still a thing—that drawer.

For a lot of us, the drawer is a norm in a home. Everyone has one, right? Well, what if I told you it is not only a shamefully, sacred space in our homes but within us as well? We are all guilty of having an inner junk drawer. It is the place we store our frustrations, hurts, guilt, insecurities, and fears right next to things that could be useful if not thrown in the mix with so many not useful things. There are plenty of dangers in mixing junk and resources; the most dangerous thing being when your resources end up getting covered in your junk because you must keep digging deep into things you should have already discarded.

In life, when we do not allow ourselves to heal from the past; every time we try to dig for assets we have to pass by the same mess. Just as you search for and finally find a rubber band but it is covered in ketchup or is too dry rotted to use, we bury our potential at the back of a drawer that becomes toxic. You start asking questions like "Am I good enough?" or "Do I know enough?" or "Do I deserve this?" or "Should I even try?" In doing so, we become frustrated before we even get to use the best parts of ourselves.

We must be intentional in what we hold on to and what we release. Just because it is a norm to many others does not mean we have to accept it as a norm as well. Protect your space and your resources. It matters more than you know. Take time to work on yourself and give yourself the chance to heal, clean up, and air it out.

day 70.

RE-UP

Isaiah 43:18-20

*But forget all that—
it is nothing compared to what I am going to do.*

*[19]For I am about to do something new.
See, I have already begun! Do you not see it?
I will make a pathway through the wilderness.
I will create rivers in the dry wasteland.*

*[20]The wild animals in the fields will thank me,
the jackals and owls, too,
for giving them water in the desert.
Yes, I will make rivers in the dry wasteland,
so my chosen people can be refreshed.*

I hope this book has helped you evaluate and establish a new perspective on things. As you work to refine some things within yourself, also take time to celebrate your fresh start. We all need to consider what it means to renew, redefine, reconstruct, revitalize, and reinvent ourselves.

By now, I am sure you know I love definitions. The prefix "re-" is used with the meaning "again" or "again and again" to indicate repetition or with the meaning "back" or "backward" to indicate withdrawal or backward motion.

Renewing something requires a reestablishment, or it calls us to resume after an interruption. To be successful in this year, check your existing foundation and what you plan to build on. Take a moment to be reflective, and identify what things became an interruption before. What plans will you make to adapt, overcome, and conquer if faced with the same adversity again?

Redefining grants the chance to define again or differently. What would you like the meaning of you to be this year? How will you exist, impact, engage, and experience life differently? Will you be a noun— person who is here and that is it? Or a verb—in action and felt?

Reconstruction occurs due to damage. Hurt is inevitable, but you cannot ignore it. You have to do the work to process and heal. Building over damage still leaves a broken interior. You have to break out the power drill to really drill into concepts, the hammer to be strong and resilient, screws to keep everything together, and the lever to maintain a healthy balance. It is a long process but one so worth it in the end.

Revitalization is THE BEST thing. After you have checked your foundations, decided the layout of you, and done the work, you become charged and filled with life. Life is meant for living and loving! It is the inspiration to inspire others to do the same time and time again.

Google defines reinvent as changing (something) so much it appears to be entirely new. Do not simply be an appearance—be an experience.

In closing, I challenge you to work on you, not reinvent you. Do not just say, "Here's the new me." Instead say, "Here's the improved me."

about the author

Bianca Chandler lives with the goal of helping people improve themselves, their lives, and the world around them. Her philosophy is simple yet powerful; "Living for impact: motivating, learning, improving, evolving."

She is an enthusiastic speaker and life coach who is dedicated to helping others. She works to help others discover and utilize how to best use their gifts by creating and providing professional development workshops, youth empowerment sessions, various seminars, and an annual woman's retreat focused on releasing and moving "Ahead."

In addition to her work helping people improve their personal and professional lives, Bianca is invested in helping people build their spiritual lives. She is a licensed evangelist and the founder and leader of LEGO Faith as well as Rooted Youth Ministry. Both are in-depth studies challenging participants to sharpen their knowledge and abilities to share the gospel.

The best you awaits!

Every Monday you can find "Minute Monday" in which Bianca provides original minute-long motivational content on www.BiancaChandler.com and on all social media platforms.

You can also visit www.BiancaChandler.com to subscribe to "Wisdom Wednesdays" for weekly inspirational content that comes right to your inbox.

post an amazon review

Please leave your feedback on reading this book.

1. Visit www.amazon.com
2. Type in the search field the book title, "70 Days, 70 Ways," along with my last name, "Chandler"
3. Scroll down, and click on "Write a customer review"

Let me know what you thought of the book and what you gained from it.

I read every review. They are tremendously helpful!

Thank you!

www.ingramcontent.com/pod-product-compliance
Lightning Source LLC
Chambersburg PA
CBHW070421010526
44118CB00014B/1856